May the most holy, God be always praised, blessed, loved, adored and glorified in heaven, on earth and under the earth, by all creatures of God, and by the Sacred heart of our Lord Jesus Christ in the most Holy Sacrament of the altar.

"This Golden Arrow," according to Our Lord when He revealed it to Sister Mary of Saint Peter, a Carmelite Nun of Tours in 1843, "will wound My Heart delightfully and heal the wounds inflicted by blasphemy."

DREAM OF THE GREAT SHIP

Dream of the Great Ship

Interpretations of St. John Bosco's Dream of the Two Columns

By Tim Bartel

Painting of the Dream of the Two Pillars in the back of the Basilica Mary Help of Christians in Torino-Valdocco, Italy

© Copyright 2005, 2007 Tim Bartel, Golden Arrow

All rights reserved. No part or entirety of this book may be used, reproduced or transmitted in any form or by any means, electronic or mechanical, including but not limited to photocopying, scanning, recording, or by information storage and retrieval system(s), or in any manner whatsoever, without prior permission in writing from the author/publisher, except in the case of brief passages embodied in critical reviews and articles.

ISBN-10: 0-9769242-0-X
ISBN-13: 978-0-9769242-0-3

Printed in the United States of America and in the United Kingdom.

Painting on back cover ©2006 Matthew Brooks (net1plus.com/users/artcatholic) Used by permission. All rights reserved.

The Catholic Edition of the Revised Standard Version of the Bible, copyright 1965, 1966 by the Division of Christian Education of the National Council of the Churches of Christ in the United States of America. Used by permission. All rights reserved.

Title design and portrait of St. John Bosco by Megan Bartel

For Becca Bartel whose dreams are like novels.

Acknowledgements

I am blessed by my beloved wife Becca Bartel for helping me find a voice, which speaks to a wider audience in this second edition. I am grateful that she never tires of the minutia of details I delve into in our conversations regarding this dream. It has been an honor to commission my daughter Megan Bartel for the title design and the portrait of John Bosco. I am indebted to Jean Anne Currivan, Robert Weigel and Mary Morris for their efforts in proof reading on various drafts. I am deeply appreciative to Vivian Morris for arranging my first speaking engagement at the completion of the first edition. Rev. Michael Mendl, SDB shared his resources of the original redactions for the dream. Jim Likoudis expertly edited pages on the Vatican Councils and storms. Thanks to Steve Lovison who focused my attention on the Dogma of the Assumption in connection with Mary's Coronation. Thanks to Ann Erwin for promoting my work in bookstores. Lastly, great thanks to publisher, patron of the youth and dreamer Saint John Bosco and to all the biographers and Salesians for preserving the documents and defending their authentic meaning and for continuing the work of their founder.

Prayer of Thanksgiving

"Blessed be the name of God forever and ever, for wisdom and power are his. He causes the changes of the times and seasons, makes kings and unmakes them. He gives wisdom to the wise and knowledge to those who understand. He reveals deep and hidden things and knows what is in the darkness, for the light dwells with him. To you, O God of [our] fathers, [we] give thanks and praise, because you have given [us] wisdom and power." ~ Adapted from the book of Daniel 2:20-23

Table of Contents

INTRODUCTION 1
THE GOODNIGHT 3
   Battle for the Youth 3
   The Supernatural 6
   The Dream 8
A PILGRAM'S GUIDE 11
   Interpretations of the Dream of the Great Ship 13
      On the cliff 13
      Vast expanse of water, Endless sea 14
      Two solid columns 14
      Immaculate Virgin Help of Christians 15
      Host of proportionate size, Salvation of believers ... 15
      Multitude of battling ships 15
      Iron prow beaks like arrows/spears 15
      Heavily armed 16
      Incendiary bombs of every kind even books 16
      Stately ship, mightier than them all 16
      Ramming the big ship 17
      Escort Fleet (flotilla) 17
      Flagship commander 17
      Very grave predicament 17
      Conferences 17
      Furious storm 18
      Flagship keeps on its course 18
      Storm rages again 18
      Helm 18
      Pope strains every muscle 18
      Anchors and strong hooks linked to chains 19
      Books and journals 19
      Breeze from columns seals the gash 19
      Unscathed and undaunted, it keeps on its course ... 19
      Blind fury 19

- Hand-to-hand combat, cursing and blaspheming ... 20
- Death and Election Coinciding 20
- Breaking through all resistance 20
- New Pope Routs Ships and Steers Between Pillars . 21
- Total Disorder – Ships founder................................. 21
- Moors.. 21
- Ships at a distance – (not the escort fleet).................. 21
- A great perfect calm now covers the sea 21
- The Main Point 21

BOOKS, SEAS AND STORMS... 25
- The Angry Sea... 26
- Book Weapons – modern philosophy as force majeure (major force) 28
  - Heading Out to Sea 29
  - Getting Sea Legs 37
- The Tide Shifts 40

SHIPS AND COUNCILS.. 43
- Ships at Sea.. 43
- The First Council 43
- The Second Council and the Course of the Church...... 44
- The True Spirit of Vatican II.. 48

THE POPE CAPTAINS 53
- Five Possibilities 53
- Theory One - A Figure of Speech 54
- Theory Two - Real Events 55
  - Iron Arrows 63
- Theory Three – Inaccurate Recordings........................ 66
- Theory Four – Yet to Come 70
- Theory Five – Conditional Paths 70
- Pope as Vicar of Christ 71

THE FATIMA CONNECTION 73
- Background of Fatima.. 74
- The First Vision... 77
- The Second Vision 77
  - Fulfillment of the Second Message:...................... 78

The Third Vision 82
  Fulfillment of the Third Message 83
  The 200 Day March 96
  Weaving a Tapestry 96
  Remedy for the Snake's Bite 98
PILLARS AND A GREAT PEACE 101
  Two Pillars 101
    Salus Credentium 102
    Auxilium Christianorum 104
  Putting an End to the End Times Theory 110
  Great Peace 116
    A Time for Peace 117
    Sabbatical & Jubilee Seasons 124
    Sabbatical 124
    Jubilee 125
    Perfect Forgiveness 126
    Sabbath Tabernacle 128
    A Biblical Triduum Prayer Vigilance 129
  Peace of Christ 130
  The Other Ships 133
  Conclusion 136
- OUT IN THE DEEP - 139
  Summary of Scribes 139
  Controversial Points 141
    Counting Popes 141
    Two of a Kind 148
    Disappearing Ink 151
    Prophetic Dream or Ordinary Parable? 161
  Conclusions About the Dream Texts 166
- RESOURCES - 169
  The 200 Day March 169
    Interpretations of the 200 Day March 171
  Litany of the Blessed Virgin Mary (Litany of Loreto) 174
- BIBLIOGRAPHY - 178

INTRODUCTION

During the writing of this book I have experienced my own pilgrimage onboard the great ship of the Church. The bonds that fasten my family and I to the pillars of Eucharist and Mary have been strengthened by the many hours spent in research and contemplation of the dream images, and by our discussions on the topic. These moments have become my treasure and I feel blessed and honored to share their fruits with you.

Although John Bosco is a canonized saint his dreams and prophecies, being in the category of personal revelation, do not necessitate Church approval. His dreams and the concepts expressed throughout this book are within the boundaries of what Catholic are free to believe. Please keep in mind that my interpretations of these dreams and visions are not intended to be perfect answers but are only one set of possibilities. Even the dreams and visions themselves may not be perfect and may come to nothing, for the church prophesies in part and when the perfect comes the partial passes away (1 Cor 13:8-10).

Peace be with you,
Tim R. Bartel

Portrait by Megan Bartel © 2006

San Giovanni Bosco 1815 – 1888

THE GOODNIGHT

John (Giovanni) Bosco was born in Becci, in the region of Piedmont Italy, on August 16th, 1815 to poor parents. His father died when John was only two years old and his mother actively assisted in his adult ministry. John spent the priestly years of his life in Turin tending to a flock of young boys whose livelihood was threatened by industrialization. He lived 73 mystically filled years until January 30th, 1888. His feast day is just one day after the memorial of his passing to eternity, January 31st.

Battle for the Youth

John Bosco's first recorded supernatural dream came at age nine. In a vision he saw children fighting and cursing. Young John rushed in trying unsuccessfully to break up the fight by force. It was then that Jesus told him that he would be able to win over these arguing children only by gentleness and kindness thus teaching them that sin is ugly and virtue beautiful. Jesus asked him to begin doing this right away. When John expressed his dismay at the prospect of such a great task for a nine-year old boy, Jesus explained that through obedience and knowledge it would be accomplished. Then He promised His mother Mary to him as teacher. When Mary appeared and held his hand the children were transformed into various animals, goats, dogs, cats, bears and more. She told John that this was his field to work in and so to make himself humble, steadfast and strong. Then the animals all turned to gentle lambs. From that point forward John knew that troubled children were to become his mission and ministry.

While still a young man John practiced and perfected many entertaining skills such as tightrope walking, tumbling, juggling and ventriloquism. These he used to entertain children. The payment for his circus acts was to attend Mass or pray with him. In June of 1841 he was ordained a priest (Don in Italian). By December of the same year he began teaching Sunday catechism and the Oratory[1] (place of prayer) began to take form. His dreams continued to be a mechanism for revealing future ministerial events.

Boys from all over came to industrialized Turin looking for work in the factories there. When the boys were sorely in need of a permanent place for prayer and worship, again he dreamt of a flock of animals. This time the animals were creating a racket so loud that it would frighten even a brave man. A Lady shepherd beckoned John to follow her and the flock. They wandered around seemingly with out aim and made three stops. At each stop some of the animals became lambs and began playing rather than biting each other. The flock grew into a large number and shepherds came, tended them and left. Then some of the lambs became shepherds. The Lady beckoned John onward to a meadow where she showed him a church with a choir preparing to play. On an instrument case he read the Latin words, which in English are "This is my house; from here will my glory go forth."

Don Bosco continued working with the boys and moving from place to place. He taught them vocations and trades so they could find jobs. He was also active in defending the rights of workers and the dignity of the laborer. Always the boys would need someplace to sleep and something to eat. They gathered together under Don

---

[1] Oratory is the name Don Bosco gave to the place where he and many young boys would gather for worship, sometimes without shelter. The term literally means place of prayer.

Bosco's direction and with little argument from the state whose opinion was that the Church should handle the problem of poverty. As long as the boys were poor and underprivileged the state was content to remand them to the Church. At times their noise disturbed the locals and they were even run off. There were cold winters but they persisted, the boys in their need and Don Bosco in his obedience.

Eventually, in another dream, the Lady showed him the exact place to build a church. She put her foot on the spot where Adventor[2] and Octavius, the glorious martyrs of the Church suffered martyrdom in Turin in 297. She said to him "on these clods soaked and sanctified by their blood, I wish that God be honored in a very special manner." Later he had another dream where the Lady pointed out a real house owned by a man named Pinardi. Mr. Pinardi rented to Don Bosco a piece of marshy property with a hayshed he would soon use as a chapel. Eventually two churches would stand on this spot, which is now marked by a golden cross. The first and small one is the Church of Saint Francis de Sales. The second and larger is a basilica that John Bosco named Mary Help of Christians.

The oratory provided a place for the underprivileged youth to gather, pray and learn. Don Bosco assisted them with their development but met with conflict as the movement toward Italian nationalization grew. Marquis Cavour, a Count who thought that such a large congregation of youth could be turned politically against his

---

[2] Also martyred was Saint Solutor. Little is known of their original story, which is lost to antiquity. The tradition of their story is connected with the legend of the Theban Legion (Benedictines). They were canonized prior to a formalized method of investigation, as was the case in the early Church for those whose intersession was a common and popular devotion.

agenda for a unified Italy, sent police to watch every move made at the oratory. His plan backfired when they returned with only good things to say. "Politics weren't even mentioned. Those boys wouldn't understand anything about politics. Now if you were to start a discussion about bread and butter, that is a subject each of them would be qualified to speak about."[3] The threat of nationalism that eventually won the political battle was all too real at times. John Bosco was constantly harassed even shot at twice.

As the boys and the clergy endured, the oratory prospered. When Don Bosco started the traveling oratory in February 1841 there were twenty boys. By 1854 there were 115 and three oratories. Six years later there were 470 boys. One year after that they totaled 600 and finally the family reached 800 or more. In 1874 Pope Pius IX officially recognized as a society the fifty priests and teachers who had been helping at the oratory and seminary. By the time of Bosco's death in 1888 there were 250 houses of the Salesian Society spread throughout the world. These homes ministered to 130,000 youths and turned out 18,000 accomplished apprentices and 6,000 priests (1200 of which remained in the Salesian Society). Today there is a thriving Salesian community on almost every continent.

The Supernatural

Saint John Bosco was seen to levitate in the air during Mass. A mystical dog he named Grigio (gray), came to his aid many times over a period of years that is far beyond the life expectancy of canines. No one knew where the dog slept nor did anyone ever see the creature eat. Saint

---

[3] Memoirs of the Oratory of Saint Francis de Sales from 1815 to 1855 The Autobiography Of Saint John Bosco, Don Bosco Publications New Rochelle, New York, 1989, Chapter 41.

Bosco could read souls, such that students would often shield their foreheads as they passed by him in an effort to conceal their consciences. He multiplied nuts, breakfast rolls and consecrated hosts. He is even said to have resurrected a boy long enough to administer last rights thereby saving his soul. But of all his unusual talents and the metaphysical, supernatural occurrences that surrounded him, John Bosco is most known for his dreams and visions. His dreams enabled him to help the orphan children of his ministry who were so marginalized by a rising industrialization and a philosophy that gave license to disregard human dignity. His dreams also foretold the future for dignitaries and laypersons[4]. They guide both the faithful and the secular seeking faith, who like orphans, are without a spiritual mother.

Saint John Bosco was grateful for the many gifts he was given because they would help him win souls. His motto was "give me souls, take away all else." To that end he instituted the Goodnight. In the evening just before curfew, one of the clergy would say a few encouraging words. It is not so different from the family practice of reading a bedtime story. The point is to teach morals and to inspire holiness. So it was on this Friday May 30 1862, that Saint John Bosco delivered in trust to the youth his now famous rendering of a dream popularly known as the Two Columns. When he told of the dream it was very much a paternal offering to the youth. They received it with awe and wonderment.

---

[4] In 1854 John Bosco predicted "great funerals at court" When he warned the King of Italy not to sign the law closing religious houses, but the king ignored his letter. On January 12, 1855 the Queen Mother died; on January 20, the Queen Maria Adelaida died; on February 11, the king's brother Ferdinand of Savoy died; on May 7, the king's youngest son died at 4 months. But that did not stop the King he signed the law anyway on May 29.

The Dream

Imagine you are with me on the on a cliff overlooking a vast expanse of sea with no other land in sight except that which is under your feet. In the middle of the endless sea, soaring to the sky, are two solid, stout columns a short distance apart from each other. One is surmounted by a statue of the Blessed Virgin Immaculate, at whose feet hangs a large placard with the inscription: *Auxilium Christianorum* [Help of Christians]. The other column, far loftier and sturdier, supports a Host of proportionate size, and underneath it is another placard with the inscription: *Salus Credentium* [Salvation of believers]. From these two columns hang many chains with hooks and anchors in every direction to which ships can be attached.

The water is covered with a countless multitude of battling ships. The prow of each is fitted with beaks of iron that are like spears or arrows stabbing and piercing everything they hit. These ships are heavily armed with cannons, firearms, and incendiary bombs of every kind, even books, and all of them are thronging and chasing after a mighty ship, bigger and taller than any of them. The enemy ships try to ram this stately vessel, to set it on fire, and to damage it in every possible way while an escort fleet shields it. All the efforts of the Pope who captains the great ship are bent to steer it between those two columns against winds and waves that favor the enemy. The commanding general of the flagship, the Roman Pontiff, seeing the enemy's fury and his auxiliary ships' grave predicament, summons his captains. All the pilots gather around the captain and hold a conference, but the storm grows steadily more ferocious, and they are sent back to command their own ships lest they founder. When it again grows a little calmer, the captain summons his pilots for a second time as the flagship sticks to its course. The enemy ships keep trying in every way to block, damage and sink the great ship. They bombard it with everything they have: firearms, cannons and incendiary bombs, the beaks of their prows, and with fire from books and journals which they try to hurl into the big ship. The storm becomes dreadful and smashes the ships of the Pope so badly that the enemies let out shouts of victory. The Pope strains every muscle continuing to steer his ship between the two columns as fierce combat ensues and all the enemy ships move in and violently ram his ship again and again. Yet all the efforts of that multitude of ships are useless as their weapons shatter, their guns and cannons sinking into the sea. In a blind fury the enemy forces take to combating the big ship with their hands, fists, books, blasphemies, and curses. Unscathed and undaunted, the flagship keeps on its course.

It is true that at times a formidable ram splinters a gaping hole or wound into the hull of the great ship but immediately, a favorable wind breezes from the two columns and instantly heals the gash and the ship continues on its way. One blow gravely injures the Pope, who suddenly falls down. Those around him immediately help him to get up, but he is struck by a second blow, falls again, and dies. Another shout of victory goes up among the remaining enemies and indescribable rejoicing is seen on their ships. But no sooner is the Pope dead than another takes his place. The assembled pilots elected another captain so quickly that the news of the preceding captain arrives with the news of the election of his successor. The enemy loses courage as the new Pope overcomes every obstacle and routs all the tottering ships with his. Breaking through all resistance, the new Pope steers his ship safely between the two columns. Once in between them, he attaches the prow to an anchor hanging from the column with the Host. With another anchor he attaches the other side of the ship to the column with the Blessed Virgin Immaculate.

Then total disorder breaks out over the whole surface of the sea. All the ships that so far had been battling the Pope's ship scatter, fleeing and colliding with one another, some foundering and trying to sink the others. Then many of the small ships scurry to the columns and attach themselves to those hooks. Some ships, which had gallantly fought alongside the great ship, are the first to tie up at the two columns. Many others, which had fearfully kept far away from the fight, stand still, cautiously waiting until the wrecked enemy ships vanish under the waves. Then they too head for the two columns, tie up at the swinging hooks, and remain there all safe and secure with the main ship and the Pope.

A great perfect calm now covers the sea.

A PILGRAM'S GUIDE

It [revelation] is not a matter therefore of intellectual communication, but of a life-giving process in which God comes to meet man. At the same time this process naturally produces data pertaining to the mind and to the understanding of the mystery of God. It is a process, which involves man in his entirety and therefore reason as well, but not reason alone. ~ Joseph Cardinal Ratzinger[5]

This chapter provides a detailed list of the images from the dream of the two columns and a suggestion of what they mean to Christians on their lifelong pilgrimage to the Father. Most of these interpretations are attainable by contemplation and require little education. These interpretations and definitions are merely the logical outcome of continuing the theme, as an active imagination will render. A biblical example of this kind of creative thinking can be found in the seventh chapter of Mark:

But immediately a woman, whose little daughter was possessed by an unclean spirit, heard of him, and came and fell down at his feet. Now the woman was a Greek, a Syrophoenician by birth. And she begged him to cast the demon out of her daughter. And he said to her, "Let the children first be fed, for it is not right to take the children's bread and throw it to the dogs." But she answered him, "Yes, Lord; yet even the dogs under the table eat the children's crumbs." And he said to her, "For this saying you may go your way; the demon has left your daughter." And she went home, and found the child lying in bed, and the demon gone. ~ Mark 7:25-30

---

[5] The Message of Fatima, Theological Commentary, Public Revelation and private revelations – their theological status

This quote occurs near the beginning of Jesus' ministry. At the center of it is the acknowledgement of the prior claim of the Jews in messianic hope. The woman must have understood, through Christ's words, the prevailing belief that Jesus was there primarily for the chosen people. Even so, she entreated the Lord while keeping within the symbolic genre that Jesus chose. In other words, she spoke in His manner of speaking and Jesus approved of it as an expression of faith. The fact that Jesus honored her response validates not only her faith but also the method she used to implore Him.

Applying this concept to the task of interpreting prophecies is simple. It is a matter of asking questions while maintaining faith that extending the theme will answer them. For instance, a good question might be: How is the great ship like the Church? To answer this we have only to think of ways that support the expressed belief that the ship is the Church. We could draw upon many writings in Catholic tradition that exemplify such a metaphor. We have the gospels themselves, which show us that some of the disciples were fisherman. We have Jesus own words saying, "I will make you fishers of men." We also have our imagination to supply us with possibilities, which we may test with more questions. Questions like: Does this fit the theme? Is there a better interpretation? Is there any evidence to show this is a wrong interpretation? Is this an improper use of the picture drawn with words?

Interestingly, the Syrophoenician woman adds a noun, an image that wasn't part of Jesus' word-picture. Still, Jesus accepted it and credited her for having spoken rightly. She added, by inference, 'table'. It stands to reason that if the children are eating a meal that was provided for them, then they must be at a table. This is nothing more than reading the implications[6]. But we must be careful not to add words that shift the meaning, words that add new symbols outside context of the story.

In general, the manner of communicating with symbols should be easily recognized as analogous to those of the dream, biblical parables, fables and similes of faith, and other prophecies. That is the gist of the way these interpretations were conceived in this chapter. All that I have done is sail along the same course in the same genre as the messenger whether by dream, simile or any other stretch of the imagination. It bears noting that God, in his infinite goodness and who has made man in his likeness, has given us the abilities both to dream and to reason for the purpose of assisting us to trust and to love him, our neighbors and ourselves. As a truth from God, both the message of the dream and its proper interpretation should teach of this trust and love.

Interpretations of the Dream of the Great Ship

On the cliff

The fact that Saint John Bosco and the students he is speaking to are not on the great ship in the middle of the battle, designates that they are removed from the events in either distance, or time (or both).

---

[6] This type of interpretation, which permits adding symbols to augment our understanding, is fair because it engages as its principle the diegesis set forth in the simile/prophecy. It begins with trust that the prophecy is authentic and comes from the mind of one who is capable of communicating meaning on more than a superficial level. Or you might say it is a hermeneutic of trust.

Vast expanse of water, Endless sea

This is the world, which is mostly water. Because the sea seeks its own level it is an instrument of justice and true equality. It was life for Noah and his family, the Israelites and all those baptized yet death for those left in the great flood and for Pharaoh's chariots. The sea became their grave. It is a barrier that wicked men cannot traverse. Revelation chapter 13 describes a beast that defies death and judgment by coming up out of the water. It also describes those who had conquered the beast, its image and the number of its name as standing on the shore of a sea made of glass and fire (Rev 15:2). When Jesus walked on the water it foreshadowed the conquering of death through the cross and resurrection. When Peter could not walk on the water he called out "Lord save me!" This foreshadowed that though Peter would abandon Jesus, he would return and strengthen the others. Peter put his faith in Jesus who helped him to stand on the water, showing that the Church's authority and power over death, through apostolic succession, is vested in Peter and rooted in Jesus, our salvation (Mat 14:23-36). The sea may also illustrate mystery because of its unseen depths. The Lord's judgments are like the mighty deep (Ps 36:7) exceeding man's understanding (Is 55:8,9).

Two solid columns

Column or pillar stands for witness and truth. Pillars often memorialize events or people. When a column stands separate that is, when it is not performing the function of holding up a roof, it is set as a marker or statement of accomplishment. The fact that these are the only two stable structures in this panorama indicates that they are grounded, have a foundation beneath the mysterious sea of faith. Since they rise up out of the sea, which we have already mentioned represents mystery and death, this means that these two pillars and what is on them transcend mystery and conquer death.

Immaculate Virgin Help of Christians

The sharing of this role in conquering death is an indicator of Mary's co-redemptive participation. Her role as "Help of Christians" points to her participation in the co-mediating of graces. Mary is help to those who are devoted to her Immaculate Heart (Approved July 21, 1855) through the rosary, which is the psalms, the word that she herself contemplated. The Miraculous Medal also approved during Don Bosco's lifetime (1830) likewise depicts Mary assisting with necessary graces for our salvation.

Host of proportionate size, Salvation of believers

Size equals importance. This column is far loftier and sturdier indicating that it is more important and more regal. Whereas Mary is the Help of Christians, Jesus is the Salvation of Christians. So this is a host of Salvation. Salvation is in the sacrifice of the Mass John 6:53-58. Since the goal and destination of the ship is the Eucharist this implies that the pilgrimage of the Church is liturgical.

Multitude of battling ships

The battling ships are institutions, organizations and nations. The enemy ships that attack the stately ship are persecutions or accusations leveled against the Church.

Iron prow beaks like arrows/spears

Iron represents technology since it is the metal that defeats bronze. Iron is also most likely the metal that the nails and spear that pierced Christ were made of.

Heavily armed

The enemy has premeditated its attack. To be armed requires production, which requires planning and time.

Incendiary bombs of every kind even books

The books are made out to be weapons since they are equated with guns. As a gun shoots a small but deadly projectile, so too these books send out tiny but potent and poisonous messages. Also used in similitude to the books are cannons and incendiary bombs, which are the kind that explode. This indicates that some books, just like some weapons are more disastrous than others. As the effect of a bomb is to scatter shrapnel and fire outward, this literature has far reaching ramifications. In the same way that the interior of bombs or explosive devices is the threatening element, it is the books content that is injurious to life and the living. This is a war of words and thoughts, philosophy, science, and ideology and all that is predicated on them.

Stately ship, mightier than them all

This is the Body of Christ, particularly the Church Militant at war with sin and temptation. The Catholic Church since stateliness and mightiness imply royalty and authority, which is descended ordinarily but also succeeded. The great ship amidst the sea also invokes the image of the ark of salvation. This is true of both Noah's ark, and the Ark of the Covenant, Mary. Lastly, the ship provides the largest grounding, something on which to stand in the middle of the ocean. One does not lean on his own understanding but relies on the word of God. The Catholic Church guards that full deposit of faith both written and spoken.

Ramming the big ship

This is a tactical maneuver of ironclad ships from antiquity. They pierce the side of the ship like the centurion's spear that pierced Christ's side.

Escort Fleet (flotilla)

These satellite ships are one with the mighty ship while they are on the same course. Their being independent of the large ship requires other captains to keep them in escort. These are the Catholic cardinals and bishops of other countries and jurisdictions who are delegated the duties, in ecclesiastical authority, of overseeing dioceses. According to the First Vatican Council[7], "... the bishops who, under the appointment of the Holy Spirit, succeeded in the place of the apostles, feed and rule individually, as true shepherds, the particular flock assigned to them. "

Flagship commander

The Pontiff – Further proof that the stately ship is the Catholic Church.

Very grave predicament

This is the spread of false doctrine, loss of souls, and onslaught of enemies.

Conferences

These are the First (1869) and Second (1965) Vatican Councils. The time line is an interesting one to interpret. There are few words in this dream occupying the space between the two conferences and yet there are nearly a hundred years between Vatican Councils. This is a strong indicator that this story is not a parable cleverly conceived but a true vision or dream. For in dreams and visions time

---

[7] Dogmatic Constitution *Pastor Aeternus* on the Church of Christ (1870)

is not expressed by the proportion of words or the duration of the image but by a series of things. This is because man experiences time in a linear way so it is best expressed to the spatial mind as a series of things that represent events. For biblical examples examine the dreams of Pharaoh (Gen 41) and king Nebuchadnezzar (Dan 2).

Furious storm

This is the Franco-Prussian War, Modernism, Romanticism, World War I. Chastisement. Consequence. Seasonal weather indicating appointed times.

Flagship keeps on its course

Never strays from doctrinal purity. The doctrine of Papal infallibility is decreed (1870 at the First Vatican Council). In view of the column with the Eucharist, the Second Vatican Council begins a reform of the Liturgy of the Mass. The reform, as designed, was on course.

Storm rages again

Second World War. Spread of communism.

Helm

This is the Vatican, or the seat of Peter.

Pope strains every muscle

Personal struggle. Physical suffering. This Pope is applying the full strength of his faculties especially his intellect, but also his heart and prayers according to the first commandment as Jesus affirms in Mark 12:29, "Jesus answered, "The first [commandment] is, 'Hear, O Israel: The Lord our God, the Lord is one; and you shall love the Lord your God with all your heart, and with all your soul, and with all your mind, and with all your strength.'" This is a Pope of single-mindedness, whose goal is the two pillars of the Eucharist and Mary.

Anchors and strong hooks linked to chains
Strong, successive links forming, inseparable bonds forged of metal not rope. The doctrines and dogmas revealed to and decreed by the successors of the apostles.

Books and journals
Ideologies, philosophies, printed words principalities not flesh and blood. This is an indication of the unseen at work in attempting to destroy the visible Church.

Breeze from columns seals the gash
Divine intervention. Holy Spirit, the breath of life, the comforter at work healing the Church where wounded.

Unscathed and undaunted, it keeps on its course
This is the promise of Christ that the gates of hell shall not prevail against the Church. Even though they are attacking the Church the course remains steady, meaning also that the documents of the Second Vatican Council are no less valid than those of the First Vatican Council. Since schismatic groups have used this dream in an effort to illustrate descent within the Church, the fact of a steady course clearly contradicts such interpretation. Instead, what is discernable is that the Church's effort to renew the Liturgy continues amid opposition and wide spread abuse.

Blind fury
The enemy cannot see, no understanding, no power (John 1:5), devil prowls about like a lion seeking whom he may destroy (1 Peter 5:8), seeking the ruin of souls (Prayer to St. Michael).

Hand-to-hand combat, cursing and blaspheming

You can't fight hand to hand if you are not onboard the ship. The enemy is in the structure of the Church, in her organization and in her places of worship. As Pope Paul VI is famed to have uttered, "Through some crack the smoke of Satan has entered the Church of God[8]." This is much like the birds that make their nest in the Church's branches from Luke 13:19. Inasmuch as these men are grappling in the sanctuary and a goal of the ship is the Eucharist, the reason for their fighting may be proper liturgical worship.

Death and Election Coinciding

Similar to the way Easter Sunday closely follows Good Friday. What this section of the dream is conveying is that the Church endures in imitation of Christ, dying and rising again. It is also an implication of the passage of time or the mark of an era (see Conference on pg 17).

Breaking through all resistance

Resistance is the Cold War. Even after the storms/wars the enemy continues to resist. It is Communism, post-modernism, and now Cultural Creativity (inventing your own heritage), and the culture of death. It is also Post-conciliar conflict, especially over the Liturgy. This new Pope in the dream is able to break through these conflicts, which may be illustrating a type of reconciliation or a decree since it is done by strength of his own initiative (like a Motu Proprio).

---

[8] This quote is purported to be from Pope Paul VI, Papal address June 30, 1972, however no document could be found at the Vatican web site.

New Pope Routs Ships and Steers Between Pillars

The new Pope successfully unifies the bishops with a view toward the Eucharist and necessarily a renewed Liturgy.

Total Disorder – Ships founder

This is the collapse of Communism in Russia and the rise and fall of nations, the fruition of the self-refuting nature of many philosophies touting man as his own god.

Moors

The Church has ordered herself to Christ and Mary. By mooring to the pillar of the Eucharist the Church has arrived at proper Liturgy.

Ships at a distance – (not the escort fleet)

This is a new springtime in the Church. It is Catechumen waiting to join the ecclesia. It is other religions, and nations slowly converting as they make their way across the aftermath and confusion.

A great perfect calm now covers the sea

This is an era of peace. It is the last day of the week. The day of Sabbath rest, when God is satisfied with His work. It is an entire season of Jubilee.

The Main Point

Similarities between the dream of the two columns in 1862 and the great battle of Lepanto in 1571 suggest that the dream is really a cleverly devised parable and perhaps lacks true prophetic character. The battle of Lepanto is well known throughout Europe and was certainly known by Saint John Bosco. So the argument that Lepanto inspired Bosco to create a parable is reasonable. However, when you look closer at some of the historical events that occurred after the dream was told, the prophetic dimensions of the dream become equally undeniable. We will examine some of the historical events throughout this book. For now let's take a brief look at the battle of Lepanto in 1571.

Seeing the grave oppression of slave Christians by Islam and the great power of their naval fleet, Pope Pius V called for all Europe to pray the Rosary and ask for victory. Under the command of Don Juan, an outnumbered Catholic armada assembled from Spain, Venice and Genoa, virtually annihilated the Muslim forces in one of history's bloodiest sea battles. Andrea Dora, Admiral in the Christian forces, carried a small copy of Our Lady of Guadalupe into battle. It is reported that at the moment of victory, hundreds of miles away in a Vatican meeting, the Pope went to the window exclaiming "The Christian fleet is victorious!" then wept, and thanked God. Shortly thereafter he bestowed upon her the title and invocation "Mary Help of Christians." To this day there are tokens pillaged from defeated Muslim ships strewn over Europe as monuments to the glorious victory attributed to Mary's intersession. The Feast of the Holy Rosary which we celebrate October 7, was originally instituted by Pope Pius V as the Feast of Our Lady of Victory in commemoration of the intercession of Mary in this battle at Lepanto. Pius also inserted a new title for Mary, Help of Christians, into the Litany of Loreto[9].

Lepanto has been used to argue against the dream's prophetic nature despite revealing post-dream historical facts, the dream's focus on the Eucharist and other dream images describing a very different kind of war. Prophesy

---

[9] This litany is also known as the Litany of the Blessed Virgin Mary.

in this dream or parable covers a period of more than one hundred and fifty years and encompasses two Vatican councils, and at least two identifiable Popes. True, the intersession of Mary in the triumphant story of Lepanto is mirrored in the dream of the great ship but is also augmented. Where the battle of Lepanto boasts of the intersession of Mary, the dream boasts of Mary and the Eucharist. Symbolically, the books used as weapons denote a battle fought with the intellect more than with faith, which signifies conflict not with nations having religious government, like Muslim forces in the battle of Lepanto, but with nations born of ideologies like Nazism, Communism and Marxism. Whether parable or prophecy, the basic message is the same; that although the ship is at war against sin and temptation an alliance with Jesus in the Eucharist and the intersession of Mary by means of the Rosary brings triumph, justice and peace.

BOOKS, SEAS AND STORMS

"Over the years I have become more and more convinced that the ideologies of evil are profoundly rooted in the history of European philosophical thought." ~ John Paul II [10]

The strangest of the dream images is perhaps the books used as weapons. They are included among other more deadly seeming weapons like guns, cannons and bombs, which means there is some inherent similarity between the books and the other weapons. This shared affinity is the potential to destroy life. What God may be trying to communicate to us through Don Bosco is the power of the written word[11], the might of the pen that empowers the sword. Bosco was actively engaged in countering the profane publications[12] of his day, with his own newsletters. He knew well, how damaging and deadly to the eternal soul the wrong words could be and how edifying the message of Christ is. So it is the content of the books that makes them a threat. Though Don Bosco did not leave us with anything denoting the content of the books, it is apparent in the philosophies and writings of his day. Individually these writings are a single weapon like a gun or cannon or bomb. Collectively they are the fuel for revolution and constitute the turbulence of the sea.

---

[10] Memory and Identity, John Paul II, Rizzoli International Publications, Inc., New York, N.Y. 2005, p 7

[11] Printed images like pornography also have a deadly effect on the soul.

[12] Reforms in Piedmont in 1847, loosened press censorship. John Bosco mentions two immoral papers that came out around this time: *Il Risorgimento* (Published by Count Cavour - nationalist), *L'Opinione* (Published by James Durando – anti clerical). These papers John Bosco contrasted with two catholic papers: *Larmonia* [harmony] and *Unita Catolica* [Catholic Unity]. The former paper changed over the decades to a militant agenda.

The Angry Sea

At the center of the angry sea, churning up waves is Europe, especially the Papal States of Italy, and the region of Piedmont Italy where John Bosco was born, lived, ministered and died. In the century preceding John Bosco the dominant foreign powers occupying Piedmont had changed hands from the Spaniards, to the Austrians and then the French under Napoleon. Late in the 1700's it was divided from Italy and became part of the Kingdom of Sardinia until the unification[13] of Italy was finalized in 1870.

The 1700's in Europe were a time of social, political and military upheaval. The French Revolution, which used the people to cause uprising, resulted in the separation of church from state. Worse than that, the revolution sought to keep Catholics from unity with Rome. During what was known as the Reign of Terror, French Government enacted laws that sold church property and deported priests. The revolution ravaged the temporal territories of the Papacy resulting in the exile of Pope Pius VI to France, where he died, in 1799. Ironically, the rise of the people empowered Napoleon to the level of Emperor, who in turn briefly restored the Papal States.

The mutual tolerance between Pope Pius VII and Napoleon, which was evident in the papal agreement to his coronation on the contingency that his marriage to Josephine be sanctified (by Cardinal Fesch; Napoleon's uncle), lasted a brief eight years. For those eight years

---

[13] Unification is a misnomer since the papal city remained independent. The term also implies that the Papal States were not unified while they were under the Papacy.

Napoleon asserted imperial authority by ruling on church appointments and imprisoned even some cardinals simply for annoying him. When in 1808 Napoleon insisted that the foreigners be banned from Papal States and that England and Orthodox Russia be barred from its seaports, Pope Pius VII refused on the basis that the Church is Catholic. That is, it is universal and so could not, as a light of peace to all nations, exclude any nation.   Napoleon responded by force, with his troops occupying Rome and the Papal States and exiling Pope Pius VII. It wasn't until 1814 when the whole of Europe rose up against him that Napoleon freed the Pope to return to Rome. That same year the allied republic exiled Napoleon.

 The badly battered Church would spend the next two decades in a vain effort to restore the piety and virtue that the modern idealism of Reason, Nature and State had relegated as irrelevant. The pendulum had swung to the far opposite side as strict social controls were enacted under Pope Leo XII (1823-9).   Restoration saw better efforts under Popes Pius VIII (1829-30) and Gregory XVI (1831-46). Then came Pius IX (1846-78). A Roman Republic revolution overthrew the papacy in 1848 for not sanctioning their rebellion against Austria.   Five months later French and Austrian troops restored Pope Pius IX who quickly adopted a new outlook toward alliances with conservative monarchs.   In those five months Rome went from one diametrically opposed declaration to another. She went from being hailed an anti-clerical democratic republic to official papal city.

 A movement known as Risorgimento lead by Giuseppe Mazzini, Giuseppe Garibaldi, Count Cavour and King Victor Emmanuel II was centered in Turin where Don Bosco ministered. Turin was Italy's capital from 1861 until

1865, because the French army guarded the preferable city of Rome. This Risorgimento movement, seeking to set up a secular state, rebelled against the power of the Church killing a brigade of Catholic defenders in the process. In 1870 the French troops that were guarding Rome were withdrawn to fight the Franco-Prussian war, leaving it defenseless against the Italian army who seized it for country and king. Now all the Papal States were fully annexed and Italy became a nation while the Papal real assets were diminished to a fortress, a lone rock protruding out above an angry sea. This is the rock on which Don Bosco invites us to imagine ourselves with him at the start of the dream narrative.

Book Weapons – modern philosophy as force majeure (major force)

The Church, a great and mighty tree that had grown from the smallest of seeds (Matt. 13:31-32; Mark 4:30-32; Luke 13:18-19), was being choked under the soil by a younger, rapidly growing weed (Compare[14] Matt 13:25-30). The roots of this yearling and the underlying dynamism of all the military, political and social upheaval are less territorial and more ideological. It was an irreligious philosophy that hailed man's power as self sufficient for his cause and purpose for being. The new century of the 1800s would become the century of the celebration of man's achievements and liberation from Church and therefore God. The industrial age was dawning and with it a philosophy of free thinkers whose trust and teaching were not in God alone but in man and nature alone or nothing at all. This ideology would evidence itself as the major force of the revolution and the voice of the secular

---

[14] The enemy sews weeds among the wheat.

people, fostering other liberation movements in the century to follow and a culture of death.

This next section, *Heading Out to Sea*, is an exploration of the ebbing away of modern philosophy. It is provided here for those readers who seek intellectual details of the philosophic descent of the 1800's. Some readers may prefer to skip ahead to the summarizing pages of this section beginning on page 37 with *Getting Sea Legs*.

Heading Out to Sea

This period of time, near the end of the Enlightenment, was a time that brought to the consciousness of secular and religious alike, many challenging questions. Ironically, it was some centuries earlier, those that had been called the dark ages, which produced illumination on these very same issues. The answers that the Church gave to these questions early on through Saint Augustine (354 A.D. – 430 A.D.) and then later through Saint Thomas Aquinas (1225 - 1224) was in this age held suspect and irrationally set aside in pursuit of so called transcendent knowledge.

Saints Aquinas and Augustine built upon philosophies established by, Aristotle (384 B.C. – 322 B.C.) and Plato (428 B.C. – 347 B.C.). They all predicated their system of thought upon the reliability of sense experience. God, being perfect goodness and being free from all evil, could not have created man with senses that deceive. So long as the senses observe their proper object[15] what information

---

[15] Optical illusions are not deceptions of the senses but the improper application of the wrong sense to the object. For instance, a spoon extending past the water line in a glass of water appears to the eyes to be broken at the water line. Is it in fact broken? If you run your finger down the side, the sense of touch will tell you that it remains whole. The proper objects of the eye, or the sense of sight, are color and shapes. And the proper objects of the sense of touch are

they gather is reliable, is truth. The Averroists of the thirteenth century when Saint Thomas Aquinas lived claimed that philosophy was independent of religion since, they demonstrated that knowledge is autonomously derived through the senses. Aquinas reconciled Augustine's human/spiritual principle with the Averroist claim. At the center of Aquinas' metaphysics are the axioms:
- ♦ All knowledge originates from physical tangible sense data and is made intelligible by the intellect, which can elevate thought to intangible spiritual realities such as the human soul, angels and God.
- ♦ Higher truths such as the Mysteries of faith require the assistance of revelation. In other words, knowledge can be both sensed and revealed.

In addition to the axioms on revealed and sense knowledge, Aquinas established five proofs of the existence of God; Motion (prime mover), Sufficient Cause, Necessary Being, Gradation, Governance of the World. The most important for our discussion is the proof from Sufficient Cause, the syllogism for which goes like this:

Major Premise:
Every being that does not have within it the cause for it's being must have its cause in another (contingent cause).

Minor Premise:
It is not possible for there to be infinite contingent causes, else nothing would ever have come to be.

Conclusion:

---

temperature, texture and depth as seen in forms like the spoon in the glass of water.

Therefore there must be a first cause, which is sufficient in it self (God).

This proof also asserts that cause and effect are connected as one. When a cause stops so does its effect stop. This is important especially when it comes to the cause of being. If our cause for being were to cease, then we would cease to be. This reinforces the Church's teaching that God is not only the creator of all things but also its sustainer.

Thomas' proof from causality went unchallenged until René Descartes (1596-1650) applied systematic (or hyperbolic) doubt to sensory perception. His goal was to arrive at certain truth by process of elimination. He hypothesized that what we perceive as sensory perception is really our minds projecting sense qualities on objects. Our existence then is a subjective perception. From this he derived the infamous "cogito ergo sum". Translated from Latin into English it means, "I think therefore I am". This became the founding of secular reasoning and philosophy. Since Descartes all philosophers begin their arguments with, the Cartesian Principle, the mistrust of sensory perception and therefore the tangible gifts of God in the world all around us.

Flash forward to the 1700's. The promulgators of the many "-isms" of the Enlightenment era disregarded the rectitude of both revealed knowledge and sense knowledge. In contrast to the apostles who were fishers of men, the thinkers of the 1700's and 1800's produced a fissure in philosophy that continues to split to this day. The number of isms of this era and the details of their philosophy are too many for the scope of this book to relay comprehensively[16]. The few that follow will however, exemplify the descent of higher thought to the dregs of man's intellect when separated for the assistance of his creator.

David Hume (1711-1776) aplied Descartes' system of doubt to causality and dismissed the tennants of cause and effect presuming instead something he called constant conjunction. In other words effect follows cause but does not share in its being. As an example, consider a train station where everyday at precisely three o'clock a whistle blows and then moments later a train pulls into the station. Hume would say that the whistle is not the cause of the train but happens to regularly and predictably coincide with its arrival. Put in syllogism form constant conjunction would read like this:

Major Premise:
Our senses cannot be trusted as accurate representation of reality.

Minor Premise:
That effect shares being with cause is a mere and untrustworthy sense perception.

Conclusion:
Therefore effect must only follow cause in a separate but predictable fashion.

The flaw in Hume's logic is clear to see in the Major premise. Hume presents the Cartesian principle of doubting perception as fact. All of modern philosophy is built upon this sandy foundation.

---

[16] For a detailed look a those persons and philosophies most responsible for orchestrating the cacophony of chaos in this present darkness see *Architects of the Culture of Death*, De Marco Wiker, Ignatius Press 2004

Immanuel Kant (1724-1804) acknowledged that this world is not self-sufficient. That is, it requires a cause and sustenance beyond itself. So far, so good. However, he considered all reality to be merely a perception and not something that exists substantively. He claimed that all reality as we know it is just the individual imposing the forms of space and time upon sensation[17]. If all that we know is what we perceive, and all reality is metaphysical (beyond the physical), then understanding the "thing-in-itself" he said, is beyond human reason[18].

George Hegel (1770-1831) claimed that all human activity is only the working of the universe as it progresses to

---

[17] Kant does not explain how perceptions appear to be universal. Surely, not every intellect would apply the forms of space and time the same way unless they were of the same nature, which means each of us was designed with a common nature. Design presupposes designer and therefore purpose. If man has a purpose then he should rightly act to fulfill it, which will require trustworthy reasoning and sensory perception. To accomplish its goal man's intellect must be able to trust his senses, which present to it the world around him. Else his experience will be false and therefore any reasoning built on trusting this experience will also be false. Thus he will only be able to fulfill his purpose in semblance but not in truth, not in actuality. For God to create man with a purpose but not endow him with the power of reason, intellect and sensory perception to reliably fulfill it is to say that God is not good. Or that he is deceptive. God cannot be evil because then it would be possible to conceive of a being with greater perfection, one in whom all goodness resides. And since God is the perfection of all things therefore God is good. Since God cannot be evil man must be able to trust his intellect and therefore his senses that interact with it.

[18] The question should arise, how did Kant arrive at this absurd conclusion? If the idea came to him from external sources, by his own definition it is merely a perception and we cannot know that it is the thing-in-itself (noumena). If the idea came to him internally, then it is derived from what he knows, which he has said is only sense knowledge (phenomena). According to Kant, it is not possible to know the noumena. So, all that we know or can conceive of is either directly or indirectly phenomena, a representation of things. Whether Kant came up with this concept from internal or external stimuli, by his own definition, it cannot be trusted to be the thing-in-itself. This means that Kant's work is self-refuting because we cannot trust it to be truth.

godhood. He postulated that reality is absolute, Mind, Reason and Spirit, that there is no such thing as the corporeal. The mind, he said, was dialectical, producing a thesis, which is followed by an anti-thesis and then synthesis. In this sense, the real (thesis) and rational (antithesis) are interchangeable and one (synthesis). Thus thought is reality and all reality merely a thought. When Hegel applied his views to history his followers split into two groups. The left became like Marx, Socialist and Communist. And the right became Empiricist and fueled Protestantism.

Arthur Schopenhauer (1788-1860) also followed Kant and added that man has no will of his own but follows an evil cosmic will, a primordial urge, which is the source of endless suffering as man acts out the increase of miseries. Schopenhauer's claims denigrate the personhood of God even lower than the level of an evil genius who submits his creation to endless pain and suffering. He concludes that that this evil will has no reason. His atheistic point of view leaves man utterly alone without a creator or purpose. Thus life is not worth living and death is the greatest virtue associated with life.

Aguste Compte (1798-1857) who founded Positivism (which turns out to be nothing other than humanism) believed that one should not question the existence of experiential phenomenon. Instead the goal of knowledge should be to describe it. He applied the scientific method to religion and expected a superior social order or civilization to progress organically from social science (Marx and Hitler had similar world visions mixed with the will to power and willfulness). Simply put, Compte's philosophy places man at the center of worship.

Johannes Muller (1801-1858) studied the nervous system and developed ideas of sensory experience that led to the concept of Indirect Realism, which teaches that what we perceive is merely an internal representation of an external reality, such that we can not know with certainty what the external reality actually is. Those that teach its principles claim that since we do not experience the world directly we therefore cannot know anything for certain. In other words, all we know is what we sense, not what is. This philosophy says that we can have no certitude about this world except uncertainty.

Charles Darwin (1809-1882) published his work on the origin of species by natural selection and evolution as a matter of chance rather than design. Providential evolution may be reconcilable with Church teaching on creation but strict Darwinism or accidental evolution contradicts the clear evidence of order in design, necessitating a designer. Worse than that Darwin applied his concept of natural selection to humans, predicting, "the civilized races of man will almost certainly exterminate and replace throughout the world the savage races"[19] This he explained as the natural order of things and thus necessary and beneficial. His work became fodder for the Nazis.

Kierkegaard (1813-1855) fought against Hegelian philosophy (relating to George Hegel's school of thought) and the church state in Denmark. However, his writings fueled Protestantism and later paved the way for existentialism. Existentialism recognizes people as a constant work of imperfection – an unfinished product but with no creator because He is eternal. Kierkegaard might say that only the temporal individual exists and is responsible for

---

[19] Darwin, *Descent of Man*, pt. 1, ch. 6, p. 201

his creation. Consequently, most existential works are studies in futility.

Herbert Spencer (1820-1903) reasoned that Social Darwinism should be the norm. Social Darwinism says that classes should remain segregated because of the rule of survival coined from Darwin, survival of the fittest, or that of natural selection.

Huxley (1825-1895) proclaimed himself Darwin's bulldog, and is credited for originating the term Agnosticism. He popularized Agnosticism as the belief that reality is always beyond human understanding, although the definition we accept today is; the belief one cannot know through reason that God exists. His public writings argue against the historical value of the Bible applying skeptical criticism as a normative basis of biblical scholarly understanding[20]. In short it means that to accurately study the word of God one must primarily mistrust it.

Nietzsche (1844-1900) said that God is dead. As a consequence, Nietzsche also taught that the meaning to life is something that humanity must provide. Thus man replaces God as self-actuator. The achievement of the state of man as god he called "uber-menchen" which is translated superman (some say over-man to avoid association

---

[20] Recently, this type of scholarship has been termed the Hermeneutic of Suspicion because it begins with mistrust rather than faith. Criticism of this sort does not begin with objectivity as it claims but with the subjective point of view that the Bible is inaccurate or has been altered to suit the motives of apostles and communities seeking a foothold in a pagan empire. To spend scholarship in skepticism is an adulterous flirtation in the mind, which ought to be engaged through faith. By it's very nature skepticism requires the suspension of faith, at least to play the advocate long enough to see his position for the purpose of refuting it. Unfortunately, playing the advocate sometimes has the adverse effect of seduction.

with the comic book character). Nietzsche slandered God and the Church, calling the God of Christianity a weak god and saying that pity for the poor (both in spirit and material wealth) is a weakness. Church doctrine and beatitudes he would label as the 'morality of the herd'. In contrast he promoted the 'morality of lords', which prizes courage, honor, power and love of danger. Morality of the herd and lords is something that is being preached in a set of very popular kids books these days. Maybe you know them, Harry Potter. Only Rowlings calls them Muggles. This philosophy echoes satanic beliefs of self-power or the will to power and the absence of God. More accurately, Nietzsche promoted the will to power as a sacred duty of the stronger man to dominate. Nietzsche spent the final year of his life in Turin loosing a battle against insanity.

Hitler (1889 -1945) and the Nazis, although not philosophers, borrowed Nietzsche's concepts of the herd and lords and the will to power and put it into action[21]. They believed they were the master race, the third race – not gentile, not Jew but uber-menchen (superman or uber-man). In the name of self-proclaimed god-man, the Nazis nearly annihilated the Jews. If they had the power they would have continued eliminating nations, peoples and races until they were the only ones left. Though the Nazis did not come into power during the 1800's, these are the philosophical underpinnings that they used as license to abuse power.

<u>Getting Sea Legs</u>
These philosophies, among others, are the popular writings of the day. They are the weapons, which

---

[21] Action is the distinguishing characteristic between the will-to-power and willfulness. What the will-to-power idealizes, willfulness actually attempts. So if racism is the agenda genocide is the result.

wrought by the mighty pen, empowered the sword. They are the books thrown at the great ship in the dream. They are the propaganda not only of that century but of ours as well. Today these false ideals of self-power, self-will, and self-love give personal license for free love, and have been argued into United Sates legislation, for the legal practice of abortion and euthanasia[22]. All of these ideals presented in these publications are built upon the sandy foundation of a false major premise and for that reason anything they conclude will inevitably implode and scuttle as the dream predicts.

In contrast to the liberation of man from God that philosophers of Modernism spread, contemporary Popes remind us of our origin in faith and dignity in the image of God. John Paul II began his pontificate in 1979 precisely where modern philosophy found its insufficient end (because it tries to redeem man by his own power). He wrote Redemptoris Hominis, which deals with the redemptive work of Christ as a demonstration to man of his dignity as a reflection of God. (He also appealed to us all to honor the Eucharist by proper examination of conscience and Penance [section 20], and also to pray with Mary [section 22]. You may recognize these as the two pillars of the dream.) Throughout his pontificate, John Paul offered the humanity of Christ as the answer to the world's failing humanisms. Where the world lost its trust in God and put its faith in man, John Paul would continually encourage us to trust in the god-man, Jesus.

One of John Paul's commissions and gifts to the Church is the Catechism of the Catholic Church. If the members of

---

[22] For a detailed examination of the development of the culture of death from liberation philosophy see *Architects of the Culture of Death*, DeMarco and Wiker, Ignatius Press 2004

the great ship in the dream also have books as weapons, the Catechism is surely heavy artillery, and along with it the Lectionary. I include the Lectionary in this category because of the unprecedented way it brings the word of God to the people in Liturgy. The lectionary not only cycles through nearly the entire Bible in three years but also emphasizes Christ's messianic mission as prophesied throughout the books of Moses and the Prophets by juxtaposing them with the New Testament readings. The Catechism belongs in this category because of the way it speaks to today's society about transcending truths.

In order to properly recognize the Catechism as the compendium of reasoned and revealed knowledge, permit me to paraphrase praises of the Catechism from George Weigel's, *God's Choice*. 'While contemporary culture claims that the origins of our religious and moral traditions are beyond reach, the Catechism gives us full ownership, teaching that the Risen Christ remains her living and faithful guard and guide. While secular intellectuals argue that the world is an unsolvable puzzle, a series of endlessly divided, unrelated and non-purposeful events, the Catechism demonstrates that the Church's teaching and faith throughout the ages is unified, interrelated and meaningful. While today's culture prefers relativism and remains skeptical of absolute truth, the Catechism explains that truth (God) is the essential and only satisfaction for the soul. While members of the fallout of western ideologies champion the accomplishments of man despite their prevailing beliefs that he has no past, is uncertain of his nature and present being, and predicts increasing cataclysmic events for his future, the Catechism praises God in the persons of the Holy Trinity for lovingly giving man his origin and history, for including him today in His plan, and for hope in the certain future that is the fruition of God's love[23]'.

The Tide Shifts

In the dream, when the storms rage, they create waves that seem to favor the antagonists. This describes a shift in popular worldviews. When the Church had power of state the predominant worldview was Christian Theism, which explained through ages of discernment and with apostolic authority, that God who is both creator and sustainer of life could be known through unaided reason. Of course we still need the Church as an authoritative interpreter of scripture (and giver of sacraments), but far from being a pompous claim, this axiom says that one does not even need the Church in order to know that God exists. To be clear, the revelation and proper teaching of who God is requires the Church but to know that God exists man needs only his gift of reason. Man knows he is not sufficient to be his own cause and therefore he must have his cause in another who is sufficient for His own cause and being. As a result, it is every person's individual responsibility to apply his own intellect and will to the understanding that God is. Acknowledging God prepares us to receive His grace in which we find our dignity. Man does not receive the power to do as he wills simply because he wills, but he receives and perceives his dignity when he wills in accordance with the power that created him. The will to power ends in destruction and death; the will to love ends in creation and life.

---

[23] Paraphrased from *God's Choice: Pope Benedict XVI and the Future of the Catholic Church* – George Weigel 2005 Harper Collins Publishers Inc. p44

By the end of the so-called age of enlightenment, and perhaps as late as the 1900's the synthesis of many philosophies emerged as the worldview and contrasted our Catholic theistic perspective. We can observe a digression or regression from this faith at that time. In Schopenhauer we see Deism, which says that God is uninvolved in the world (even though Schopenhauer would not acknowledge a divine creator with personhood). In Kant we recognize Fideism, which says that except through grace reason is not capable at arriving at knowledge of God's existence. In Nietzsche, Atheism (non-existence of God) and Rationalism (man as the measure of all things). Philosophy had attempted to liberate itself from the jurisdiction of God and wed relativism to willfulness. This self-proclaimed, self-made and self-purposed world deemed God immaterial, and the message of His Church obsolete. It also gave limitless license for the willful to commit crimes against humanity on an immense and possibly immeasurable scale. This is what happens when morality is stripped of absolutes and accountability; man tries to justify his means by the end that he wants to achieve and that end is never realized. It can never be realized that way because good can never come about through evil. At least man cannot do it alone.

SHIPS AND COUNCILS

Ships at Sea

There are several sets of ships mentioned in the dream texts; the enemy ships, the great ship, the escort ships, and allied ships. The great ship is the Catholic Church. That much is easy to see since its captain is the Pope the prime disciple and bishop of Rome. The escort fleet represents the other disciples of Christ, the bishops around the world. They are in other boats to show they act independently but in unison with the great ship. The last group of ships is the allies who had fought along side the great ship and wait at a distance till all is safe. These ships may be the other Christ-professing faiths, or they may be secular groups seeking conversion like catechumen and candidates for the faith. If so, when they join the great ship at the pillars of Mary and the Eucharist, it is much like a new evangelistic springtime in the Church.

The First Council

The first time that the captains meet it is because the Pope sees the grave predicament the whole fleet is in. This describes the reason for the First Vatican Council. At this time there were strong oppositions to the authority of the papacy and the other bishops. One of the dogmatic constitutions of the council, *Pastor Aetemus*, expressed the proper weight of the hierarchy, "… the bishops who, under the appointment of the Holy Spirit, succeeded in the place of the apostles, feed and rule individually, as true shepherds, the particular flock assigned to them. " This constitution assists us to see the dream as correctly depicting the image of the auxiliary ships and captains as bishops. Though they are independent they are one with the big ship.

The Franco-Prussian War pre-empted the council just the way the storm in the dream raged so heavily that the captains were sent back to tend to their ships and keep them from foundering. But the storm hardly settles before the Pope is moved to bring the captains together again for another council. This may indicate that the Second Vatican Council was intended as a conclusion to the First Vatican Council.

The Second Council and the Course of the Church

During the Second Vatican Council the world's claim that God, the Church and their message are irrelevant came to the forefront. The resulting documents expressed the proper relationship of the Church to the world and encouraged the development of new ways to tell an age-old story without compromising the truth of it. Unfortunately, what developed were two contrasting points of view[24]. The first is an infiltration of the modernist axiom; any and all change is good. The second is a reactionary stance that no change is good. The truth is not necessarily a humanistic (or Hegelian) synthesis of these two and is not necessarily located somewhere in the middle. The truth resides with the real spirit of Vatican II, which has yet to be fully received and realized in the new order (Novus Ordo) of Mass.

What the Fathers of the Council encouraged were new ways of conversing with the present modern culture

---

[24] A number of good things developed from Vatican II as well. One perhaps deserving better mention than this footnote is the Lectionary, which not only cycles through nearly the entire bible in three years but also emphasizes Christ's messianic mission as prophesied throughout the books of Moses and the Prophets by juxtaposing them with the New Testament readings.

(Aggiornamento[25]) and in light of the Church's patristic roots (Ressourcement[26]) but the consequent modernism that took place without concern for Christian roots was to the Church's detriment. While some in the council wanted to radically reform the liturgy others, including Joseph Ratzinger, wanted the new liturgy to be in continuity with the original mold. This would have been more a recasting rather than a radical reforming, which would connote distorting the mold. Unfortunately, the "changes" that were implemented in Western countries without magisterial approval, and are still in practice almost everywhere, betray a false Aggiornamento rather than any true Ressourcement. This false Aggiornamento and false understanding that the new missal authorized creativity was expressed in the rationalization that it was the "spirit of Vatican II." A fact that belies this excuse is that it had to be expressed as a spirit because it cannot be found anywhere in the letter of Vatican II[27]. Pope Benedict XVI explains that this misunderstanding, "frequently led to deformations of the liturgy which were hard to bear.[28]" Consequently they leave the faithful craving the recovery of sacrality in the Eucharistic celebration.

It is an understandable reaction to this infiltration of modernist tendencies disguised as "the spirit of Vatican II" to follow the pendulum to the far right. Unfortunately that is where some Catholics succumbed to serious errors and even to schism. This is where we find Sedevacantists

---

[25] Aggiornamento is an Italian theological term that literally means "bringing up to date"
[26] Ressourcement is a French theological term that literally means "return to the sources" or to source again.
[27] Some will argue that *Sacrosanctum Concilium* section III D: 37 is an invitation to admit cultural truths found outside the Mass. However, these adaptations must be approved as section III D: 40:1 expressly reads.
[28] Letter by Pope Benedict XVI accompanying the Motu Proprio *Summorum Pontificum*, July 7, 2007

who believe that the seat of Peter is vacant, or the Society of Saint Pius X who refuse to accept the Novus Ordo rite. An excellent resource on this topic is "The Pope, The Council and the Mass " by James Likoudis and Kenneth D. Whitehead, Emmaus Road Publishing.

From a purely prophetic point of view, the Church remained on course after Vatican II since the ship in the dream remained on course after the second storm and meeting of captains[29]. This is important because it means that the Novus Ordo as written is not something that sets a new course. Pope Benedict XVI is very clear on this saying that the law of prayer expressed in the missals of Pius V (Traditional Mass) and Paul VI (Novus Ordo) "will in no any way lead to a division in the Church's 'Lex credendi' (Law of belief)."[30].

Truly there are some legitimate differences between the two forms of the same rite, but the liberty to creativity is not one of them. Certainly, when we seek to change the Mass to suit our own interests we individually end up off course separating ourselves further from our origin and the great ship of our faith, which leaves little to distinguish us from worldly ideologies and practices (or from protestant forms of worship) whose doctrine continually fractures. To make the Holy Mass into something of independent, modernistic imagining without concern for the true apostolic understanding is to diverge from the image and design of Christ. Such additions and subtractions from the liturgy of the Word and the Eucharist can only lead to division, which is a scandal against the Church's holy and indelible mark of unity. It pits progres-

---

[29] Ironically, this dream of the Two Columns is often used by Sedevacantists to illustrate descent in the church, yet there are no such images.
[30] Motu Proprio *Summorum Pontificum*, July 7, 2007, Article 1

sive Catholics against orthodox Catholics. Anyone can witness this empirically in just about any Catholic parish worldwide (particularly in the United States). Without debate, the Liturgy should not be used as license to fracture the body of Christ by either side, whether by intention or by omission. Neither should the hopes of either side justify any lack of charity in this debate.

O.K., so the "reform of the liturgy" failed to meet man where he is, does that mean that we should "Reform the reform" by another council? There is a certain tendency to want this. However, trying to reform the reform this way might just press harder on the fault line in the hull of our church/ship and it threatens to do as much damage as repair. But there is a better reason why we do not need another council to reform the reform; the form of the Church is perfect the way Christ made her and consequently the ongoing development of His liturgy is proper as the council and the Popes defined it. Instead of *re*form, what the Church needs is to *con*form to her original character, condition and mode. Reform means to form again (re- means *again* in Latin). Conform means to form with or in accordance with (con- means *with* in Latin). It is all of us who need to conform to the way Christ instituted His Church and His Liturgy to grow. It is the whole Church that should moor itself to this pillar of the Eucharist, Christ who is the salvation of believers[31]. Conforming to proper liturgical prayer is the way we will reach the pinnacle of actual participation in worshiping God.

---

[31] This may be what John Paul II wanted us to consider in the new Luminous Mysteries of the Holy Rosary, especially at the Mystery of the Institution of the Holy Eucharist.

The True Spirit of Vatican II

In summary, there is bad news and there is good news. The bad news is that the non-conforming philosophies of the culture of death have grown inside the body of Christ like a cancer forming and reproducing its own non-conforming cells. The good news is that the true spirit of Vatican II, the Holy Spirit can and wants to heal this great ship that is the Church in the new millennium. The ship that is battered with holes, that appears to be a fractured church, can receive the breath of God as a favorable wind of healing and new life. That is why, taken directly from the dream imagery, the real spirit of Vatican II is the Holy Spirit. In order to realize the great gifts of healing and renewed life (springtime) in store for us we need to be open to that Spirit and humble ourselves, returning to the sacraments and to prayer, dedicating ourselves to those same two pillars to which the disciples devoted themselves while adhering to authentic teaching in community; the breaking of the bread and prayers (Acts 2:42). Just as the problem is two-fold (radical change and progressive spirit) so too is the solution two-fold, devotion to both Jesus in the Eucharist and Mary through the Rosary[32].

What then is the Eucharistic goal of the Church in relation to the world and what are we saying by steering that way? Are we just trying to stamp out heresy or are we praying even for our enemies? Initially, yes the Church was concerned with combating heresy, but eventually she came to deal with the world. Archbishop Fulton Sheen expresses it well in his nineteen-seventies retreat titled Priest as Victim:

---

[32] Contemplating the Luminous Mysteries unites both these devotions in proper context and is an act of mooring to those two columns.

"Today the great concern is the world around us. It is ecological as it were. It is the environment in which the Church lives. It is the world and what is to be our attitude toward it. The Vatican Council for the first time in the history of the Church discussed the world. That was chapter thirteen.[33]"

The images of the Dream of the Great Ship depict a similar war between the Church and the world. They pertain to this present age where the forces of light and dark, good and evil are engaged in war. The Church was always at enmity with the world but especially so since Vatican II. That is when the Church reinforced that the world is the object of its mission of conversion. To which the world has violently responded, 'get your nose out of our business!' We should expect this much, "for sin has diminished man, blocking his path to fulfillment[34]." But the Church does not leave the world alone; rather it seeks to gather to His flock as many as will come. The Church's message to the world has not changed in two thousand years, only the way in which it conveys that message. Perhaps because the message remains unchanged, the modern world thinks the Church is not relevant. As an example consider how Europe struggles to make a unifying constitution but vehemently denies the Pope's request to include only one sentence recognizing Christianity as a formative force in Europe's history. Saying that the Church has no relevance for today or no place in the modern world because it is two thousand years old is like saying that a tree's branches have no place in the sun because its roots are in the ground.

---

[33] There is no thirteenth chapter in any of the Vatican Documents. He may be referring to item 13 of chapter 1 in *Gaudium et Spes* [Pastoral Constitution On The Church In The Modern World], which deals with the dignity of man through his suffering in the light and knowledge of Christ his redeemer.

[34] *Gaudium et Spes*, Chapter 1 number 13

The Church is a living Church, its traditions living traditions, its scripture living words, its sacraments living sacraments, such that she lives through time and space always existing in the past, the present and the future, always having meaning and purpose in that space and time which stems from its beginning not just as a seed but from the life it was given by the one who planted it and continues to nurture it. A living being, whose source is life itself, must always have both the reason and the relevance for it's being because of and in that source at all times. That source, that life is the Eucharist. Officially, the Church is clear on what her renewed celebration of the Eucharist ought to be. In practice there is conflict. How can this church, which Christ made to be in peace with God, make peace with the world if it cannot make peace within itself? Once we conform to the proper form of the Novus Ordo Mass this Church will once again become salt and light to the Earth. Just as in the journey of Jonah[35] our storm will only abate once the sacrifice we offer is the one that Christ instituted. This kind of unity amongst us and in the most Holy Mass will be one sure sign that Christ gave us as part our four indelible marks; Unity, Holiness, Universality, Apostolicity.

It is the Lord in the Eucharist who sustains the Church and it must be the Lord from whom and to whom she relates her life and purpose. If we return to Him, He will give us the Holy Spirit and a new Pentecost. In the Spirit we could preach Christ in modern terms, with words and compassion that compel modern thinkers and doers to take notice. But detaching the desire to bring the Church into a modern dialog with the secular world (aggiornamento) from the source of Christianity (Ressourcement) is

---

[35] See the Holy Bible, the book of Jonah 1:14-16

like a bride divorcing her groom on the wedding night. It is an annulment, a nullifying act. It is Christianity without Christ, a Christ-less cross. Therefore any movement to bring the Church up to date must maintain its connection to its roots, must maintain the perspective and principles of its beginnings. Without this life sustaining connection to its roots the Church in the modern age would not be a ship on course, she would just be a piece of driftwood.

THE POPE CAPTAINS

Don Bosco's biographer Fr. Lemoyne expressed that we should let events prove the veracity of the dream. This is excellent advice even if it requires patience while waiting for its full fruition. We have already seen how the great ship represents the church and the tempest represents the age of post-'enlightenment'. The setting then is Don Bosco's own lifetime and the conclusion is a moment of peace since a perfect calm covers the sea. That this perfect peace is yet to be seen is not likely to be argued so let us accept that it describes a future event. If we seek to know whom the Pope-captains of the great ship are we should begin with the saint's own lifetime then continue forward looking for facts that fit the story's progression. We hope to find facts for all the elements of the dream yet we must acknowledge that there could be a problem with the texts, the translation, or our understanding and interpretation of them. It is sufficient to leave some things to mystery but those things we understand must fit historical fact if we hope to maintain that the dream is prophetic.

Five Possibilities

There may be innumerable variations of interpretations for this dream yet there are five larger categories under which they might fall. We will examine each of these categories within this chapter. It should also be noted that the truth might be in any combination of these simultaneously in the same way that scripture can have multiple levels of meaning. This is not meant to elevate this dream to the level of scripture but to recognize the same Holy Spirit still at work in the mystical body of Christ, since we are not left as orphans.

The categories are:
1. A Figure of Speech - The dream is depicting a figurative and general injury and death like Pius IX confined in the Vatican.

2. Real Events - The dream is derived from real events that become symbols representing a real Pope.

3. Inaccurate Texts - The redactions of the dream were not recorded accurately enough and with enough detail in this area to find a perfect fit with history.

4. Yet to Come – Events have yet to unfold which will fulfill this prophecy perfectly.

5. Conditional Paths – The two Popes who fall once each are not two consecutive Popes but one Pope whose future is uncertain.

Theory One - A Figure of Speech

How could the dream depict a figurative injury and death? In his Address on the Dreams of Saint John Bosco, given at the Eucharistic-Marian Congress (approximately 1997) Reverend Mike Mendl answers the question. "If we wish to interpret the Pope's first fall in Don Bosco's allegory, and then of his second, fatal fall, we might explain it this way: The first fall represented the temporary overthrow of the Pope's temporal power during the Revolution of 1848, when Pius the IX was driven into exile for about a year and Garibaldi, Mazzini, and their friends set up the short-lived roman republic. The fatal second wound might represent what many people could foresee in 1862: that the Church's temporal power would be taken away completely in the future, as happened in 1870. From that "fatality," a new kind of Church leadership emerged."

This is an interesting application of the dream images, which equates the health and mortality of the Pope in the dream with the condition of the Church's temporal power. This fits the dream nicely since the next Pope in the dream was elected without the prior Pope having been restored to health first. We should consider that although the Pope is "helped up" the restoration of the Pope's health is not a focus of this dream and so neither is the condition of the Church's temporal power a focal point. There just aren't enough details to be conclusive.

This interpretation begins by retrofitting the dream of 1862 to the year 1848 and the exile of Pius IX, which relocates the dream out of the realm of prophecy and regards it as a parable. So how do we handle Don Bosco predictive interpretation of the enemy ships? He is recorded to have said that the enemy ships, which cause the fall of the Pope "represent persecutions that are in store for the Church. What has happened up to now is almost nothing.[36]" Following Fr. Mendl's tract of thought would mean that when Don Bosco said this he was conjecturing, making an educated guess. For this reason, this idea of a figurative death and election of Popes works best if one considers the dream to be an allegory constructed from perceptible events of the era.

Theory Two - Real Events

The problem of identifying the Popes in the dream is that not all accounts agree. According to Fr. Lemoyne the four written accounts agree with each other about the number of Popes while they contrast a single surviving

---

[36] *Don Bosco's Dreams* by Pietro Stella, translated by John Drury, Salesiana Publishers, Boggero letter, p78

oral account of Cannon Bourlot, who was at least twice a visitor to the oratory. Bourlot is recorded to have insisted that there were two Popes who fall and thus three Popes in total (see the last chapter Out in the Deep for a detailed exploration of the testimonies). So the question arises; is it one Pope who falls twice or two Popes who fall once each? Either way Papal history should provide us with proof or else we must be content for the future to play out the roles and actions that the dream expresses. Yet what if, in history, there is neither one Pope who falls twice nor two Popes who fall once each? Then what? Would there be cause to doubt the accuracy of the texts or should we rethink our interpretation and expectations? Consider that in the 1860's, many at the oratory suspected that Pope Pius IX (1846-1878) was the Pope of the dream and expected to see in their lifetime both an attempt at his life and then his assassination. They were happily mistaken including Canon Bourlot.

Pope Pius IX was considered a liberal in his pastoral years because he advocated administrative changes in the Papal States[37]. As Pope he immediately gained popularity among the Nationalists when he enacted some practical reforms setting up city and state councils. However, this popularity was short lived as he made it clear that he had no intention of establishing a constitutional state since he believed that the temporal sovereignty of the Holy See was indispensable to its spiritual independence. For the decade of 1860 the revolution confined him to the Vatican under the protection of the French army. In 1868 he decreed it forbidden for Catholics to partake in a political life of the usurping kingdom of Italy. Pope Pius IX has to

---

[37] The Oxford Dictionary of Popes by J.N.D. Kelly, Oxford University Press 1986, p. 309

his credit several major contributions which the Church treasures including:

- Defining the Immaculate Conception of the Blessed Virgin Mary (1854).

- Calling for a return to Thomism and denouncing the 'principal errors of our times' with special attention to the fallacious argument that the Pope 'can or should reconcile himself to, or agree with, progress, liberalism, and modern civilization.' (Quantra Cura, Syllabus of Errors 1864)

- Consecration of the Catholic world to the Sacred Heart of Jesus (1875)

- Summoned the First Vatican Council (1869- 1870)

All of these events made Pope Pius IX suspect by Nationalist standards and therefore a prime target, however he was not assassinated. In fact, his is still the longest papal reign encompassing 32 years from 1846 to 1878. In the three years after he died devotion to Pio Nono (Literally Devout Ninth) increased but did not prevent a rabble faction of anticlerical fascists from attempting to throw his body into the Tiber River while in transit to his final resting place.

By the time Bourlot revisited to the Oratory in 1886 for the first time since the telling of the dream, the First Vatican Council had already been concluded for about fifteen years and Pope Leo XIII was already engaged strongly in refuting socialism, communism, nihilism and free masonry, making him a prime target also. According to the dream Bourlot, like many others, would have expected this Pope to be the one who falls. But history wouldn't have it.

By the time Bourlot returned to the Oratory (in 1907) for the second time since the dream, Pope Leo XIII had passed into eternity. At that time Pius X was Pope. It had been 45 years, three Popes, and a revolution since the dream had been told and while the general combatant theme of it was being fulfilled, the assassination of a Pope was as yet unrealized. Had Bourlot and the others heard right? Had they understood the meaning of that part of the dream? After such a long period of time this topic remained a hot one in the Oratory. All of the historical events gave Don Bosco ample motive and recourse to allow and even encourage controversy over Bourlot's version of the dream in hopes of stirring prayer and devotion for the sake of the Pope and the Church and for individual piety. This he had done previously and recently with success (as noted in the last chapter Out in the Deep; i.e. the story of the grim reaper shrouded in gray that comes unexpectedly for the boy in the playground). No doubt, this is what Don Bosco would want from us today as well. For there has been no historical event that literally, absolutely and precisely fits the story as Canon Bourlot expressed it.

But what about a single Pope who falls twice? How many Popes between 1862 and present fit this description? Has there been a single Pope who was injured in an assassination attempt even once? So far there are eleven to examine. Let's start at the beginning with the Pope who reigned at the time the dream was told.

Pius IX (1846-78) - After the murder of Minister of the Interior Count Rossi in 1848, Pius IX fled into exile in Gaeta (north of Naples). With the help of French troops he was restored to Rome in 1850. In 1870 he called the First Vatican Council but the garrison that protected him were called to fight the Franco-Prussian war. Italy, which had become a unified country over those two decades, advanced and occupied Rome. Pius IX was offered personal inviolability through the Law of Guarantees, but it would have been at the cost of the papacy and all its successors. His refusal resulted in his imprisonment in the Vatican for the remainder of his pontificate. Although some consider this the first injury to the papacy, no attempt was ever made on his life directly.

Leo XIII (1878-1903) - Crowned in the Sistine Chapel because the Italian government feared an uprising. Although Leo maintained Pius' ruling that Catholics could not be active in the political life of the usurping country of Italy, his life was not in immediate threat.

Pius X (1903-14) - Although he opposed the Law of Separation, which proposed to return church property in exchange for her "independence", Pius X was not in immediate danger. His death coincided with the outbreak of World War One. As a humble and holy man, there were miracles associated with him and he was canonized a saint in 1954. No attempt was ever made on his life.

Benedict XV (1914-22) – A man of peace, Benedict proposed a seven-point plan to end war through justice rather than military triumph. His plan was rejected, primarily because France and Britain ignored it. He was allowed no part in the peace settlement of 1919. He died of influenza at the age of 67. No attempt was ever made on his life.

Pius XI (1922-39) – Pius XI negotiated the Lateran Treaty with Benito Mussolini, which recognized Italy as a

Kingdom having Rome as its capitol. In return the Vatican became an independent, neutral state. As the threat of communism increased, Pius condemned atheistic communism in his encyclical *Divini Redemptoris*. National Socialist Germany at first seemed to provide security for the Vatican through a concordat agreement. Soon the Nazi government broke the concordat repeatedly and Pius issued the encyclical *Mit Brennender Sorge*, which denounced Nazism as fundamentally anti-Christian. Pope Pius XI was clearly an enemy to the Nazis and Communists yet no attempt was ever made on his life.

Pius XII (1939-58) – Using the reasonableness of natural law, he called for an immediate and lasting peace from all nations. He did not endorse Hitler's attack on Russia even though he considered communism a much more dangerous threat. Major encyclicals of his include: *Divino Afflante Spiritu* (treats on modern historical methods of biblical scholarship), *Munificentissimus Deus* & *Adoneli Reginam* (Both on the bodily assumption and coronation of the Blessed Virgin Mary), *Mystici Corporis Christi* (Mystical Body of Christ). No attempt was ever made on his life.

John XXIII (1958-63) – With the vision of a new Pentecost, John XXIII called the Second Vatican Council. He died after the first session of the council. He was loved by many people of many nations, and had few if any enemies. No attempt was ever made on his life.

Paul VI (1963-78) – Reconvened the Second Vatican Council uninterrupted. Set up post-conciliar commissions. Major encyclicals include: *Humanae Vitae* (Human Life – Regulation of Birth), *Mysterium Fidei* (Mystery of Faith – Eucharist). Known as the Pilgrim Pope for his many travels. Although the Vatican denied the event, the

Associated Press reported in November of 1970 that Pope Paul VI was stabbed by a "dagger-wielding Bolivian painter disguised as a priest" while in the Philippines Manila Airport. There is no further information available on this topic, which leaves it unsubstantiated and tends toward its improbability and irrationality. It may have been leaked to the Associated Press as a prank.

<u>John Paul I (1978)</u> – In his inaugural address to the cardinals he announced his intention to follow through with Vatican II initiatives while at the same time maintaining "intact the great discipline of the church in the life of priests and of the faithful." He was the first Pope to dispense with the usual coronation. His pontificate was very short and his death surrounded by conspiracy theories. Most of these theories hinge on the fact that Pope John Paul I was embalmed the day after his death without an autopsy. Oddly, the number three recurs when reviewing his time as Pope. He was elected on the third ballot. His inauguration was held on September third. He died three weeks after the inauguration just thirty-three days after election. He was found at 5:30am in bed with personal papers and the light on, which brings up the question; was the actual time of his death 3:30am? This theory is speculative at best.

<u>John Paul II (1978-2005)</u> – George Weigel describes John Paul II as a man of single-mindedness in the biography *Witness to Hope*. One story from the book that exemplifies this comes from his youth as a playwright and actor. During one clandestine performance, while he was acting, a Nazi loudspeaker began broadcasting propaganda but he never stopped speaking even though no one could hear him over the din. This is characteristic of John Paul's integrity. He rejected the threat of evil while focusing on

goodness. In this respect John Paul II is much like the Pope in the dream who uses all his strength to steer the ship.

John Paul was elected to the papacy by nearly unanimous vote and became the world's first Slavic Pope. He too declined the traditional coronation and accepted the title "universal pastor of the church" and fulfilled his vision to be a "witness of universal love[38]" to the world. On May 13, 1981 he was shot twice at close range. Four bullets were fired and he sustained critical injury to his abdomen and chest just a few millimeters from his heart. In 1983 John Paul II met with and forgave his assailant Mehmet Ali Agca, while Agca was in prison[39] in Rome. John Paul II wrote many encyclicals far beyond the scope of this book. Preaching peace, trust and solidarity throughout his pontificate and offering the humanity of Christ as a solution to the century's worldly humanisms. In his later years and on the world stage, he endured Parkinson's disease, which was truly a witness for life while the problem of euthanasia escalated. His was a walk with Christ on the path to the cross.

Benedict XVI (2005-Present) – Born on the Vigil of Easter, Benedict sees his own situation and Christian history as being "on the threshold of Easter but not yet through the door.[40]" Choosing the name of Benedict would seem to imply affinity with Benedict XV, who was the one men-

---

[38] Spoken on October 18, 1978 to ambassadors, The Oxford Dictionary of Popes by J.N.D. Kelly, Oxford University Press 1986, p. 327

[39] After nineteen years he was extradited to Turkey for other crimes. On January 12, 2006 he was released from prison and hours later Justice Minister Cemil Cicek ordered review of his case. He remains free while an appellate court reviews his case.

[40] *Salt of the Earth: Christianity and the Catholic Church at the end of the Millennium,* Peter Seewald, Ignatius Press 1997, p43

tioned above to have attempted to implement a plan for peace in Europe. It is therefore reasonable to hope that Benedict XVI, who is also a man of peace, will put forth his own plan to bring us through the door to the joy and peace of Easter. And if he is successful he will be the Pope in the dream who unites the Church to the pillars of the Eucharist and the Blessed Virgin Mary. To date, no attempt has been made on his life (thank God). May the Lord sustain him.

So there are only a few Popes whose life synopsis could be stretched to fit the incidents of the dream as it has been relayed to us. First there is Paul VI who was allegedly stabbed in the Manila Airport. Then there is John Paul I who was allegedly poisoned after only thirty-three days in office. Of course, there is John Paul II whose injuries were witnessed the world over. Popularly, John Paul II is seen as this Pope and captain, who though injured, struggles single-mindedly to navigate the ship of the Church toward safe harbor. A similarity of character certainly supports it but is there anything in the dream imagery to corroborate?

Iron Arrows

There is a detail about the enemy ships that may at first seem incidental but after exploration points to the Pope in the dream as an archetype of Christ and then by reason to John Paul II. Two of the surviving written accounts (Chiala and Ruffino) of the dream read that the prows of the enemy ships end in "a beak of sharp iron that pierces" whatever it hits. The remaining surviving account (Boggero) reveals that each of the enemy ships has "a sharp beak like an arrow at the front end." So in putting these two together, what we know is that the enemy ships are at least partially made of *iron* and that they resemble *arrows*, which *pierce* whatever they hit. We also know from the same sections of each testimony that their aim is to hit the larger papal ship by ramming it.

Although there is no mention, in any account of the dream, that the papal ship was made of wood, the tactical maneuvers in the battle described are those that were used against wooden ships[41] in antiquity. Knowing that Don Bosco's goodnight talks would sometimes last over an hour, there are bound to be some details left out[42]. Also, it is entirely unnecessary to mention such details as are commonly known contemporarily. By context we may infer that the great ship that represents the Church was made of wood. What does that tell us about the ship? Wood is obtained from a living organism and requires the work of human hands to form it into a vessel. Wood is also the material of the fishing vessels used in Saint Peter's trade. It was also the wood of a tree upon which Jesus was crucified. The very foundation of Christianity is this wood, which we must also work at carrying as Christ did if we are to follow Him. (Incidentally, the name Bosco translates to 'wood' but is best expressed in the plural form 'woods' meaning forest.)

Iron is a material better known from a previous age named after this metal, the Iron Age. When the secret of iron was learned those that knew its technology usurped

---

[41] The painting that follows the title page of this book comes from the basilica, Mary Help of Christians that Don Bosco founded. The artist and whoever commissioned the work must have also considered the great ship to be made of wood. Likewise, Mathew Brooks paints the picture on the back cover illustrating the great ship made of wood and the enemy ships with beaks of iron.

[42] Fr. Lemoyne records the very same thing in the pages directly after the dream of the two columns narrative: "A talk lasting half an hour or, at times a whole hour naturally had to be summarized. Some phrase may have gone by unheard or forgotten. Furthermore, as mental fatigue set in doubts may arise concerning the sequence of events." *The Biographical Memoirs of Saint John Bosco* by Fr. Giovanni Lemoyne, Salesiana Publishers, p 109

those who only had the knowledge of the softer metal bronze. So iron was the material that defeated bronze in battles of the sword and spear. Accordingly iron represents technology and science, while wood represents faith. In this dream it is the iron ships that pierce the wooden ship in an attempt to destroy it, just as iron nails pierce the flesh of Christ into the wood of the cross in an attempt to destroy love and life. Symbolically, the battle fought with iron against wood is a battle of science and technology pitted against faith. It is a battle of man's achievements and false sense of self-sufficiency railing against the redemptive work of Christ.

Attacking love, life and the Church is not only man, but also "the spiritual hosts of wickedness in the heavenly high places" (Ephesians 6:12). John Boggero chronicled that the prow beaks of the enemy ships were fashioned like arrows. In the Old Testament, the word most commonly translated as arrow actually has a much broader definition, 'a piercer' in a Hebrew dictionary. It is what these prow beaks, shaped like arrows, are doing that divulges to us the evil works of men and devils. These ships are ramming the big ship, ripping gashes in her side just as the spear pierced Jesus' side on the cross. It may have been one of these blows that caused the Pope of the dream to fall. Boggero records, "It is true, he said, sometimes it [the Pope's ship] was struck with serious blows, that it was also seriously hit and suffered momentary damage, but a favorable wind coming from the two columns quickly restored it. One blow gravely wounds the Pope, who falls down." In this context, it is the strike of the enemy ships piercing the hull of the great ship that hurts the Pope so gravely.

It's no secret that John Paul II was shot while in the Vatican square, much like the Pope of the dream is at the helm when he falls. But more remarkable than that is where in his body John Pall II sustained injury. Though the gunman shot four times he hit John Paul in the abdomen twice (His right arm and left hand were wounded as well). It was his side that was pierced by the bullets, like modern day arrows, darts or spears. In his book Memory and Identity: Conversations at the Dawn of a Millennium, John Paul referred to the attempt to assassinate him as "one of the final convulsions of the arrogant ideologies unleashed during the twentieth century.[43]"

In conclusion we can see that the Pope in the dream mirrors John Paul's character. Not only that but we can see John Paul's injuries as a type of piercing, much like the injured Pope of the dream. This is not the only prophetic reference to bullets that are really arrows, which pierce a great bishops side the way the spear pierced Christ's side. We will see this in greater detail in the next chapter on the Fatima connection.

Theory Three – Inaccurate Recordings

A point that one of the texts makes about the death of the Pope is that the new Pope is elected while the captains are still assembled, presumably at the second council. This means that the Pope dies while the second council is in session. If you will excuse the pun, this is a dead give away. Pope John XXIII convened and presided over the first session of the Second Vatican Council and Pope Paul VI reconvened and presided over the last three.

---

[43] *Memory and Identity*, John Paul II, Rizzoli International Publications, Inc., New York, N.Y. 2005, p 166

If the Pope in the dream is understood to fall not from an assassination attempt but from combat in general we might make a case for John XXIII succumbing under the weight of his papal office. One of the original dream redactions does, in fact, record that the Pope falls because of the blows of the enemy ships ramming into the great ship. In this case the peace that comes over the waters after continued resistance may be understood to be the end of the cold war.

What about Benedict XVI? It seems that the death of John Paul II and the election of Benedict XVI coincided. Couldn't the dream be speaking of these two? In a general sense maybe but factually it cannot be substantiated. To see this all we have to do is look at the Interregnum. That's the period of time between the death of a Pope and the election of his successor.

The interregnum consists of three stages, the Novendiales (nine days), preparation for the Conclave, and the Conclave itself. The Novendiales is a prescribed period of mourning lasting nine days. Temporarily pre-empting the nine days and occurring within the first four days, is the funeral. In the case of Pope John Paul II the Novendiales was preempted by the funeral and a few days viewing of the casket. Preparations for the Conclave and the Conclave itself have no set minimum duration. So these are two areas that can vary the most. Yet, no conclave has lasted longer than five days in the past two hundred years (see the chart on the next page). Since the telling of the dream in 1862 Papal Interregnums have ranged from 14 to 20 days with none of them having the characteristic of the death of one Pope coinciding with the election of his successor.

Pope	Elected	Died	Interregnum	Conclave
Pius IX	06/06/1846	02/07/1878	13 days	2 days
Leo XIII	02/20/1878	07/20/1903	15 days	4 days
Pius X, St.	08/04/1903	08/20/1914	14 days	5 days
Benedict XV	09/03/1914	01/22/1922	15 days	2 days
Pius XI	02/06/1922	02/10/1939	20 days	4 days
Pius XII	02/03/1939	10/09/1958	19 days	3 days
John XXIII	10/28/1958	06/03/1963	18 days	2 days
Paul VI	06/21/1963	08/06/1978	20 days	2 days
John Paul I	08/26/1978	09/28/1978	18 days	3 days
John Paul II	10/16/1978	04/02/2005	17 days	2 days
Benedict XVI	04/19/2005			

If anything it is technology that brings us the news so rapidly and with twenty-four hour coverage, that it gives the impression of a singular event between the death of one Pope and the election of another. This peculiarity of the coinciding death and election is more in line with the fact that Easter Sunday closely follows Good Friday than it is with any event in the past century. What this section of the dream is conveying is that the Church endures and that she follows the passion of Christ; dying and rising as one event lasting only a few days.

It is also possible that surviving texts of the dream narrative are recorded with the events out of order. I heavily suspect this is true. Finding the missing text on the dream that was written by Secundus Merlone might just clear up everything. Secundus' other texts prove him to be a superior recorder of Don Bosco's stories (see the last chapter Out In The Deep). This is what I hope to find in the Merlone text should it ever surface:
- Mention of a flotilla escort
- Mention of the storms
- Mention of two meetings of captains
- A Pope who dies while the captains are at council. This would correspond to Pope John XXIII.
- A different Pope who suddenly falls and immediately dies. This Pope's death would coincide with his own election (not with the election of another Pope.) This would correspond to John Paul I.
- Another Pope who falls or is struck down only once but is immediately helped up and recovers (not a single Pope who falls twice). This would correspond to John Paul II
- Still another Pope, the very next Pope who moors the ship to the pillars of the Eucharist and Mary

All of these elements exist in the redactions that we have yet they are oddly mixed into one or two Popes. I believe this is not the fault of the prophecy or of the prophet but of those who recorded it. John Bosco's biographer, Fr. Lemoyne writes in volume VII of The Biographical memoirs of Saint John Bosco, "A talk lasting a half hour or, at times, a whole hour naturally had to be summarized. Some phrase may have gone by unheard or forgotten. Furthermore, as mental fatigue set in, doubts might arise concerning the sequence of events… This of course increased the obscurity of a matter unclear of itself, especially if it concerned the future… Some claimed that the popes who successively commanded the flagship were three not two."

Theory Four – Yet to Come

The next option we have to consider is that some the events told of in the dream have yet to be fulfilled with perfection. This category is a dangerous one since it leaves us open to wild ideas about the threat of assassination for a Pope in the future. It opens a door to copycats. God forbid! Besides, we would have to ignore all the other clearly fulfilled images mentioned throughout this book. The fact that this is an area in the dream where the light of understanding is overshadowed by a dark cloud may be a reflection of the general confusion over the publicly unsolved mystery surrounding the names and organizations responsible for the assassination attempt against John Paul II[44].

Theory Five – Conditional Paths

What if the stories that John Bosco witnessed in his sleep that night were showing two distinct possibilities of the future? The one that we lived through is the one where the Pope (John Paul II) is instantly helped up after being struck. Many other prophecies have been foretold using conditional elements. And what Saint Paul said is true, we only prophesy in part (1 Cor 13:9). Could looking at the dream as presenting two conditional and possible outcomes tell us something about Christ? Yes, it tells us that His mercy is great. It tells us that He highly values the free will He gave us so that we might choose to participate

---

[44] Although the Italian Parliament named the military of the former Soviet Union as the culprits the Vatican has declined to agree.

in the divine life, thereby making our destiny with Him. But mostly, it tells us how we ought to act when confronted by a world that hates us. As we will see in the following chapters, John Paul II attributed his recovery from the gunshots to the direct intersession of Mary, saying that he "halted at the threshold of death." This halting may illustrate a crucial moment at the crossroads of two paths, one involving his sudden death and the other involving his suffering. The one he chose and which we witnessed was the long road of grief, the Via Dolorosa[45].

Pope as Vicar of Christ

Take a close look at the Popes, the martyrs and the faithful who in imitation of Christ have paid with their lives to keep the truth alive. This is the root of Christianity. This is what the dream depicts by the violence that the Pope and the great ship endure. And as it journeys to the pillars of the Eucharist and Mary amid this violence it reveals its Christi-centric purpose through a language of suffering. Because of Christ, all things, especially suffering have their meaning in the fact that He conquered sin and cast out the prince of this world so that we might be restored to the Father. Catholicism says to a war torn world that not only did Christ die so that we could have life but that life is given to us in the sacraments, especially the Eucharist. If we dwell too much on who the Pope is we risk missing the whole point. We miss Christ. So who is the Pope in the dream? He is all of them at once, and he is especially that one who reminds us most of Jesus.

---

[45] Via Dolorosa means "way of grief" or suffering. It is also known as Via Crucis meaning "Way of the Cross". It can refer to both the method of expiating sins through anguish and the actual path on which Jesus carried the cross on the way to His crucifixion.

THE FATIMA CONNECTION

"...Man himself, with his inventions, has forged the flaming sword."~ Joseph Cardinal Ratzinger[46]

Recall the story of the Syrophoenician woman (Mark 7:25-30) mentioned in the first chapter. It will help us to avoid another kind of misinterpretation concerning this present age. If the woman were to take Jesus' words at face value only, it might have lead to misunderstanding. In the literal sense dog means dog, table means table and children means children, etc. She then, might have said something like, 'what are you talking about? I'm not interested in dogs and tables and food. And the only child I am interested in is my daughter. Please heal her.' If she reacted this way what kind of response do you think she should expect from Jesus?

Taking this symbolic figure of speech literally, misses the point, which puts the speaker in a position requiring further explanation and effort. In the previous chapter we saw how the Pope in the dream can be the symbol of Christ. Symbols communicate concepts more efficiently than words, even to the point of understanding a culture. Imagine what volumes of commentary have been written on something as small as the Parable of the Sower, or the Prodigal Son. That's why it is said, 'a picture is worth a thousand words'.

Attempting to apply a strict literal sense to John Bosco's dream while still expecting something prophetic could

---

[46] *The Message of Fatima*, Theological Commentary, An attempt to interpret the "secret" of Fatima

prove to be a labor, the fruit of which is debatable. It would mean that someday the Pope will be on a ship and that his enemies attack him. Since historically, we have a modern Pope who was shot, the tendency would be to see this as affirming the literal sense, except where he falls twice. While some of this at first may seem plausible, what do you do with the giant pillars? Are we to expect literal columns to rise out of sea, one with a Host and another with a statue of Mary? Is it right to apply a literal sense to part of the dream but not all of it? The task at hand then, is to find the right interpretation of the Pope who is struck (not necessarily shot) and who falls, rises and falls again and dies. This must be done within the boundaries of the idiom of the dream while at the same time conforming to events that have occurred since it's telling. We happen to be blessed with other images from Church approved visions at Fatima. Images from these visions seen by a young girl named Lucia at Fatima Portugal in 1917 will support our argument that the Pope who falls in St. Don Bosco's dream of the great ship is John Paul II. These images of Fatima will also describe the role of Mary in salvation history. Those readers who are already familiar with the messages of Fatima may want to skip ahead the section titled *The Third Vision* on page 82.

Background of Fatima

Between May 13 and October 13, 1917, on six separate occasions, three young shepherd children Lucia, Francisco and Jacinta saw visions of the Blessed Virgin Mary. She came to the little village of Fatima, Portugal and showed these children three separate images as messages from God for the world. The faithful, and even a large part of the secular world became concerned with two questions arising from the second and third messages. In fact, many are still preoccupied with these questions today:

1. Has Mary's request for the consecration of Russia to her Immaculate Heart been fulfilled as requested in the second message?
2. What is the content and meaning of the third message, which was kept entirely secret from the world until May 13, 2000?

Accompanying the three visions was a miracle in which an astounding 70,000 people saw the sun dance in the sky and then plummet to the Earth. Francisco and Jacinta died in 1919 and 1920 while Lucia lived until February 14, 2004 as a Carmelite nun. On occasion she has provided answers to questions surrounding the miracle and message, especially regarding the fulfillment of Mary's request for the consecration of Russia to her Immaculate Heart.

Sister Lucia wrote down the content of the vision images and published the first two over four memoirs, but the vision infamously dubbed the "third secret" remained hidden. She initially divulged that secret to the Bishop of Leira, Portugal, in January 1944 at the directive of The Most Holy Mother. The Bishop in turn confided the secret to the papacy under Pope Pius XII where it remained secretive, under the Pope's discretion with the proviso from Sister Lucia that it not be revealed before 1960. Each succeeding Pope has had the opportunity to read the secret and decide whether or not to disclose its content and meaning publicly. On August 17, 1959 Pope John XXIII read and returned the third secret document to the Holy Office retaining its secret. Likewise, on March 27, 1965 Pope Paul VI read it, deciding not to publish it. In May 1967 Pope Paul VI visited Fatima and met with Sr. Lucia. On May 13, 1981 directly following the assassination attempt John Paul II asked for the third secret. Before reading it he composed and recorded An Act of Entrustment[47], which was broadcast and celebrated in the Basilica of Saint Mary Major, Rome on June 7, 1981. On July 18, 1981 upon his recovery, Pope John Paul II read Sister Lucia's original document in Portuguese and its accompanying Italian translation. He also met with Sr. Lucia on three separate occasions. He made a pilgrimage to Fatima on the anniversary of the first vision May 13, 1982 to thank the Blessed Virgin Mother for saving him from assassination at which time he reaffirmed the entrustment. On 25 March 1984, in Saint Peter's square, the site of his shooting and the Holy Seat of Peter, Pope John Paul II, with spiritual union of the Bishops of the world, consecrated the entire world to the Immaculate Heart of Mary. Russia collapsed around 1990 and communism was dealt a heavy blow. Again he met Sr. Lucia in 1991, on the 10th anniversary of the shooting. Then he met with Sr. Lucia, for the last time for the beatification ceremonies of her friends Francisco and Jacinta Marto on May 13, 2000, again on the anniversary of the first apparition. At that time Pope John Paul II released the third secret and the news made front-page headlines.

---

[47] "*Mother of all individuals and peoples*, you know all their sufferings and hopes. In your motherly heart you feel all the struggles between good and evil, between light and darkness, that convulse the world: accept the plea which we make in the Holy Spirit directly to your heart, and *embrace with the love of the Mother and Handmaid of the Lord those who most await this embrace*, and **also those whose act of entrustment you too await in a particular way.** Take under your motherly protection the whole human family, which with affectionate love we entrust to you, O Mother. May there dawn for everyone the time of peace and freedom, the time of truth, of justice and of hope" ~ Vatican Website: (emphasis is original)
http://www.vatican.va/roman_curia/congregations/cfaith/documents/rc_con_cfaith_doc_20000626_message-fatima_en.html

The First Vision
   Our Lady showed us a great sea of fire, which seemed to be under the earth. Plunged in this fire were demons and souls in human form, like transparent burning embers, all blackened or burnished bronze, floating about in the conflagration, now raised into the air by the flames that issued from within themselves together with great clouds of smoke, now falling back on every side like sparks in a huge fire, without weight or equilibrium, and amid shrieks and groans of pain and despair, which horrified us and made us tremble with fear. The demons could be distinguished by their terrifying and repulsive likeness to frightful and unknown animals, all black and transparent. This vision lasted but an instant. How can we ever be grateful enough to our kind heavenly Mother, who had already prepared us by promising, in the first Apparition, to take us to heaven? Otherwise, I think we would have died of fear and terror.

The basic message:
 Hell is the real and utterly horrific consequence for sins not forgiven. Mary's purpose for showing these children this image must have been for good so is there a fruitful reason for it? The terribleness of the imagery begs us to ask how can we keep our selves from falling into the snares of the devil? The answer to both these questions is that the child visionaries took consolation in Mary's promise to guide them to heaven. Just as in the Dream of the Two Columns it is Mary's intercession and assistance that helps them continue. This is a major point of both the dream and the first vision.

The Second Vision
   We then looked up at Our Lady, who said to us so kindly and so sadly: "You have seen hell where the souls

of poor sinners go. To save them, God wishes to establish in the world devotion to my Immaculate Heart. If what I say to you is done, many souls will be saved and there will be peace. The war is going to end: but if people do not cease offending God, a worse one will break out during the Pontificate of Pius XI. When you see a night illumined by an unknown light, know that this is the great sign given you by God that he is about to punish the world for its crimes, by means of war, famine, and persecutions of the Church and of the Holy Father. To prevent this, I shall come to ask for the consecration of Russia to my Immaculate Heart, and the Communion of reparation on the First Saturdays. If my requests are heeded, Russia will be converted, and there will be peace; if not, she will spread her errors throughout the world, causing wars and persecutions of the Church. The good will be martyred; the Holy Father will have much to suffer; various nations will be annihilated. In the end, my Immaculate Heart will triumph. The Holy Father will consecrate Russia to me, and she shall be converted, and a period of peace will be granted to the world".

Fulfillment of the Second Message:

World War One ended in 1918, within a year of the vision. Seven years later, on December 10, 1925 Mary fulfilled her promise by returning and asking the world, through Sister Lucia, for the First Five Saturdays devotion in reparation for sins:

"Have compassion on the heart of your Most Holy Mother, covered with thorns, with which ungrateful men pierce it at every moment, and there is no one to make an act of reparation to remove them."

And:

"Look my daughter, at my Heart, surrounded with thorns with which ungrateful men pierce me at every moment by their blasphemies and ingratitude. You at least try to console me and say that I promise to assist at the hour of death, with the graces necessary for salvation, all those who, on the first Saturday of five consecutive months, shall confess, receive Holy Communion, recite five decades of the Rosary, and keep me company for fifteen minutes while meditating on the fifteen mysteries of the Rosary, with the intention of making reparation to me."

On June 13, 1929 Our Lady appeared to Lucia saying:

"The moment has come in which God asks the Holy Father, in union with all the bishops of the world, to make the consecration of Russia to my Immaculate Heart, promising to save it by this means. There are so many souls whom the Justice of God condemns for sins committed against me, that I have come to ask reparation: sacrifice yourself for this intention and pray."

Also that day Our Lord said:

"They did not wish to heed My request. Like the King of France, they will regret it and then do it, but it will be late. Russia will already have spread her errors throughout the world, provoking wars and persecutions against the Church. The Holy Father will have much to suffer."

On January 25, 1938 the unknown light of the Aurora Borealis (northern lights) was unprecedentedly seen across Europe. The very next year, while Pius XI was Pope, World War II broke out. The good were martyred throughout Russia and her territories of occupation during the reign of Communism. Behind the iron curtain one could be instantly shot for making the sign of the cross in public. The request for consecration of Russia went virtually unattended until John Paul II was shot in 1981.

About the shooting John Paul said, "One hand fired; another guided the bullet.[48]" This experience with Mary's intersession at the threshold of death halted him and immediately he asked for the third secret of Fatima and entrusted the world to the Immaculate Heart of Mary by radio broadcast. In this act John Paul is like the good son who changed his mind and did the work his father asked (Mat 21:28-31[49]). Recovering, he again consecrated the whole world while in Fatima in 1982, and finally the third time in St Peter's square in 1984. Russian communism fell in 1990 but not before spreading her errors into China, and elsewhere, where true Eucharistic services must be preformed underground. The Pope himself suffered greatly from the wounds of his shooting and from Parkinson's disease, but with the resignation and the passion of a true follower of Christ and His cross.

As for the prediction of the annihilation of various nations, there are, at the time of this writing, almost forty wars and conflicts around the globe. Does this constitute annihilation? Perhaps not in the strict sense of the word yet these countries are devastated and the wars aren't over yet. Does this mean that our Holy Mother Mary's immaculate heart is at the point of triumph? That may be true. In which case, the conversion of Russia and a period

---

[48] André Frossard is credited with having first quoted the Pope here.
[49] What is your opinion? A man had two sons. He came to the first and said, 'Son, go out and work in the vineyard today.' He said in reply, 'I will not,' but afterwards he changed his mind and went. The man came to the other son and gave the same order. He said in reply, 'Yes, sir,' but did not go. Which of the two did his father's will?" They answered, "The first." Jesus said to them, "Amen, I say to you, tax collectors and prostitutes are entering the kingdom of God before you. ~ Mat 21:28-31

of peace would be proof. So, is Russia being converted? More specifically, is Russia being converted through the Church's individual and corporate prayers, along with the Pope's cooperation in consecration? While the Catholic Church is not strongly present and perhaps not that welcome in the new Russian Federation, the Eastern Orthodox Church, has restored faith to many. "In the dozen years that [Eastern Orthodox Archbishop] Anastasios has been in Albania, he has not only resurrected the Orthodox Church but also inspired a bitter, brutalized people," writes Nicholas Gage of Parade Magazine. Anastasios has most closely done for Albania what Carol Wojtyla (JPII) did for Poland in the Communist aftermath of WWII.

The Eastern Church is our closest cousin and shares our deep devotion to Mary although they may not agree with the development of Marian dogma since the split (Immaculate Conception 1854, Assumption 1950). Here is what Unitatis Redintegratio (Decree on Ecumenism) from the Documents of Vatican II has to say about the Eastern Church. "Patriarchal Churches... pride themselves in tracing their origins back to the apostles themselves." And "Similarly it must not be forgotten that from the beginning the Churches of the East have had a treasury from which the Western Church has drawn extensively in liturgical practice, spiritual tradition, and law. Nor must we undervalue the fact that it was the ecumenical councils held in the East that defined the basic dogmas of the Christian faith, on the Trinity, on the Word of God Who took flesh of the Virgin Mary. To preserve this faith these Churches have suffered and still suffer much." The Eastern Church continues to participate in this suffering indicating that they are not completely severed from the body of Christ.

The Western Church, in the fullness of time, will surely lead the children of Russia to a deep unity with Christ as dialog between East and West continues with hope ebbing toward unification. However, the time to pray for Russia's conversion is not yet over as the Catholic Church being in rightful possession of the fullness of faith, and its Pope who is the Vicar of Christ being in rightful possession of the keys of Peter, has yet to be received there with complete openness. Prayers, especially the Rosary will help bring about the full conversion of Russia. Since it was the Catholic Pope to whom their devoted Mother Mary appealed at Fatima for Russia's consecration, it can only be the church of that Pope to which they must belong. For if they love Mary and Mary acknowledges the Pope then they must also acknowledge the Pope.

Lastly, what remains to come is the time of peace that will be granted to the world. The moment of triumph may be close at hand and so the world still needs our prayers, especially the Holy Rosary. The Dream of the Two Columns emphasizes Mary's role in sharing graces necessary for conversion in much the same way. In the dream Mary has the title Help of Christians. In the Second Vision Mary promises that same help by means of consecration and prayer.

The Third Vision
[Lucia continues writing, this time about the third vision:]

After the two parts which I have already explained, at the left of Our Lady and a little above, we saw an Angel with a flaming sword in his left hand; flashing, it gave out flames that looked as though they would set the world on fire; but they died out in contact with the splendor that

Our Lady radiated towards him from her right hand: pointing to the earth with his right hand, the Angel cried out in a loud voice: 'Penance, Penance, Penance!'. And we saw in an immense light that is God: 'something similar to how people appear in a mirror when they pass in front of it' a Bishop dressed in White 'we had the impression that it was the Holy Father'. Other Bishops, Priests, men and women Religious going up a steep mountain, at the top of which there was a big Cross of rough-hewn trunks as of a cork-tree with the bark; before reaching there the Holy Father passed through a big city half in ruins and half trembling with halting step, afflicted with pain and sorrow, he prayed for the souls of the corpses he met on his way; having reached the top of the mountain, on his knees at the foot of the big Cross he was killed by a group of soldiers who fired bullets and arrows at him, and in the same way there died one after another the other Bishops, Priests, men and women Religious, and various lay people of different ranks and positions. Beneath the two arms of the Cross there were two Angels each with a crystal aspersorium in his hand, in which they gathered up the blood of the Martyrs and with it sprinkled the souls that were making their way to God.

Fulfillment of the Third Message

At the conclusion of a solemn Mass of John Paul II in Fatima in 2000, Cardinal Angelo Sodano addressed the public prefacing the nature of the third message and its proper interpretation:

That text contains a prophetic vision similar to those found in Sacred Scripture, which do not describe with photographic clarity the details of future events, but rather synthesize and condense against a unified background events spread out over time in a succession and a duration which are not specified. As a result, the text must be interpreted in a symbolic key.

Cardinal Angelo announced this at the directive of the Holy Father. By so doing John Paul II has restricted all manner of interpretation of the third message to the symbolic. It is apparent that his motive for doing this is to alleviate any fear the public may experience in misinterpretation, so that all those theories, which he could foresee imagining the literal assassination of the Pope by a military force, could be averted. Problematically, John Paul himself has made literal interpretations of the vision, equating himself as the bishop with halting step. This is not to be viewed as a contradiction but an exercise of his authority. In obedience, we will therefore examine the symbols of this third message as wholly symbolic except where John Paul has provided more specific meaning.

Some of these interpretations have greater relevance to the Dream of the two Columns than do others. Yet I have included all of them as they may interest the reader.

The Fiery Sword

The Bible helps us to understand the fiery sword. The first place in the Bible that we read about this sword is at the fall of man.

...therefore the LORD God sent him forth from the garden of Eden, to till the ground from which he was taken. He drove out the man; and at the east of the garden of Eden he placed the cherubim, and a flaming sword which turned every way, to guard the way to the tree of life. ~ Genesis 3:23-24

Here the fiery sword and the angel are the instrument and enforcer of God's judgment respectively. They are protecting the tree of life. Think of what fire and sword do. The blade is used to enforce judgment, to bring about justice and to defend in times of war, while fire consumes the matter it burns. The symbol of a fiery sword would then describe judgment and destruction by war for the sake of protecting the tree of life, which is the truth. It is a defense against blasphemy and desecration. This fits with what Mary said in the second vision that if the offense against God continued another war would break out.

In the writing of this third vision, Lucia mentions that the flames flashing from the sword looked as if it would set the world on fire. The angel seems to be intent on administering judgment and justice, which may imply the angel's anticipation of judgment and chastisement by war. We may also view World War I and World War II, along with many other wars, to be the chastisements Mary mentioned in the second vision. In this sense the third message is warning us of the just recompense for sin. How great the chastisement could have been, since the angel's flaming sword did not touch the Earth in the vision yet in reality we were visited with many wars. The devastation could have been much worse. How great then is Mary's intersession and Jesus' mercy!

In the Dream of the Two Columns the war that encompasses a large part of the narrative is also connected with judgment since the enemies weapons backfire and their ships scuttle and sink. This is also fitting with scripture since the flood and the sea are how God enacted his judgment for people of Noah's day and the army of Pharaoh in the Exodus. The parallel between the third Fatima vision and this dream is not found between fire and flood but in war.

Radiating Splendor

When our Holy Mother puts out her right hand and the light emanating from it outshines the fire of the angel's sword, she is interceding to prevent or postpone the impending chastisement.

Here Mary is clearly pictured interceding. The light that comes from her hand is much like the rays of light that are seen emanating from rings on her fingers in the image of the Immaculate Conception on the Miraculous Medal. In the vision the rays of light seem to be a manifestation of mercy. In the Miraculous Medal the rays of light are graces that she wants to give to believers. This ties in very well with the dream of the Two Columns, which describes Mary as both the Help of Christians and the Virgin Immaculate[50]. While it is true that the placard written below the column with the statue of Mary reads, "help of Christians", yet two of the three surviving original texts and Fr. Lemoyne's biographical memoirs refer to the statue atop the pillar as "Blessed Virgin Immaculate" or "Immaculate Virgin". So, in this dream we have an interesting synthesis of the two Marian devotions such that picturing either image atop the pillar would be appropriate. What encourages me to give priority to the Immaculate Conception image is that the Dogma of Immaculate Conception was promulgated only eight years prior to the telling of the dream.

Thrice Penance

The angel points to the Earth with his right hand and cries out penance three times. Instead of the full wrath of

---

[50] Mary Immaculate was the focus of Don Bosco's Marian devotion up to this period of his ministry where it begins to revert back to Help of Christians as it had been in his youth.

God through fire and sword that we deserve, the word that we are given is penance in the superlative form. This is a perfect decree, not a recommendation. In the English language we have adjectives for describing degrees of things. For example, good, better and best. The angel's words accomplish the same superlative through repetition, the way it is done in Hebrew or Latin. Saying the word one time is ordinary, twice is strong, and three times is perfect, maximum or superlative. The world has been given a chance to repent and to do penance to avoid chastisement. This is similar to the major point of the dream. In the dream it is not about penance so much as devotion evidenced by the ship tied to the pillars. Yet the overall point is the same. The relentless enemies of the ships that is the Church sink to the bottom of the sea and this is like non-repentance. In the end some ships stay far off till the waters are safe, then they advance to the two columns. Their caution may be an indicator of an examination of conscience that precedes repentance.

Immense Light

The immense light that is God represents all good, all truth, all confidence and all knowledge since this great light would eradicate all shadow. Shadow would represent evil, lies, doubt and false understanding. The light of God conquers all things. In the dream that light, which conquers, is substantiated in the Eucharist and we can see this when attaching to it brings peace.

As in a Mirror

Since God is in the position to see the events on Earth and this part of the vision directly follows Mary's intersession, this reflection shows the events that will follow as a result of that act of mercy. They depict the triumph of her immaculate heart as described in the second vision. What immense authority has been given her by heaven that even God the Father yields to her intersession! Truly hers is a heart perfected like that of the Father.

The Way of the Cross

It is interesting to note that this third vision does not directly depict apostasy. With something like a great mirror we might expect to see our selves in our sinful state. Instead it shows those holy men and women, religious, priests, bishops and the Pope making a holy pilgrimage toward salvation in imitation of Christ. Which brings to mind the words of the Communion Rite at the sign of peace:

> ...Look not on our sins, but on the faith of your Church...

Here the Lord shows us the holy ones of our time whose selfless acts atone for the sins of others. We see that, as Cardinal Sodano wrote regarding the Third Secret, "It is an interminable Way of the Cross led by the Popes of the twentieth century[51]."

In Don Bosco's dream there is also a pilgrimage, not up a hill but across a vast sea, not to a cross but to the Eucharist. In both the dream and the vision Christ is the main focus and the journey to him is perilous.

Bishop Dressed in White

The bishop, who is the Pope, is dressed in white to show his purity. It also shows him as a martyr. This we derive from Revelation chapter seven:

---

[51] Address Of Cardinal Angelo Sodano Regarding The "Third Part" Of The Secret Of Fatima At The Conclusion Of The Solemn Mass Of John Paul II, Fatima, 13 May 2000

"After this I looked, and behold, a great multitude which no man could number, from every nation, from all tribes and peoples and tongues, standing before the throne and before the Lamb, clothed in white robes, with palm branches in their hands, and crying out with a loud voice, "Salvation belongs to our God who sits upon the throne, and to the Lamb!""
~ Rev. 7:9-10

"…These are they who have come out of the great tribulation; they have washed their robes and made them white in the blood of the Lamb." ~ Rev. 7:14

In keeping with the symbolic interpretation we should rightly consider that this Pope must represent something beyond himself. To do less would be inconsistent. So let us for the moment, view the Pope of the vision as an archetype of all Popes. Let us say that he represents every Pope or at least those of the twentieth century. Joseph Cardinal Ratzinger concluded the same:

In his arduous ascent of the mountain we can undoubtedly see a convergence of different Popes. Beginning from Pius X up to the present Pope, they all shared the sufferings of the century and strove to go forward through all the anguish along the path which leads to the Cross.[52]

As we have already seen in the previous chapter, the collective Popes of the dream typologically represent every Pope.

---

[52] *The Message of Fatima*, Theological Commentary, An attempt to interpret the "secret" of Fatima, Joseph Cardinal Ratzinger, Prefect of the Congregation for the Doctrine of Faith

The Rough Hewn Cross

This is the type of cross which is depicted at the top of the papal staff used by Popes Paul VI, John Paul I, John Paul II, and now Benedict XVI. This cross is not prepared in advance but made of rough wood in haste. It shows the fact that Jesus' trial was concocted and rushed unfairly. His trial and judgment came so fast and was so unexpected by the Romans that even they who were skilled at such torture were caught ill prepared. A cross had to be made on the spot to carry out His death sentence. This is an indicator that God is expedient to provide justice and mercy through His holy martyrs. The trunks being rough also have greater semblance to the tree from which they were taken and therefore illustrate that Jesus was crucified on a tree. This tree, with Christ on it is the tree of life:

"But Peter and the apostles answered, "We must obey God rather than men. The God of our fathers raised Jesus whom you killed by hanging him on a tree."" ~ Acts 5:29-30

The cross with Christ on it is the sign of sacrifice. In the dream the pillar with the Eucharist is the same sacrifice. In this case the connection between the third secret and the dream is not readily apparent but requires catechism.

The Half Ruined City

This is the home that man has made for himself, the theatre of our world and is the paradox of Christianity. Whether it is in this condition from the aftermath of war, the decrepitude of age, or the incompetence of the men who built it is not explicit. It very well may be the literal destruction of civilization by war. What is expressed though is that this city is presently devastated. Symbolically, figuratively, this Pope walks through the valley of the shadow of death. This is the culture of death that John

Paul II spoke of in his homily on August 15, 1993 at World Youth Day, Cherry Creek national Park, Denver Colorado.

This marvelous world - so loved by the Father that be sent his only Son for its salvation (cf. Jn 3:17) - is the theater of a never ending battle being waged for *our dignity and identity as free, spiritual beings. This struggle parallels the apocalyptic combat described in the First Reading of this Mass (Rev 11:19, 12:1-6,10). Death battles against Life: a ``culture of death'' seeks to impose itself on our desire to live, and live to the full.*

And:

The paradox of the Christian message is this: Christ - the Head - has already conquered sin and death. Christ in his Body - the pilgrim People of God - continually suffers the onslaught of the Evil One and all the evil which sinful humanity is capable of.

The destruction in this city is much like the scuttled enemy ships of the dream.

Halting Step

In the midst of his own pain this Pope prays for the souls of the corpses he meets along the way. Even though the third message has a symbolic nature, it is plain to see that this Pope if he may represent a single Pope is John Paul II. In his own personal journey to God the Father, John Paul II was witness to so much senseless killing by the Nazis and after that in the cold war. He suffered from Parkinson's disease and still traveled the world canonizing more saints in his lifetime than have been canonized in all prior centuries combined[53]. This Pope of the Third Secret

---

[53] *John Paul II is History's Champion Saintmaker* By Cathy Lynn Grossman USA Today, 2005

of Fatima, who stops to pray for the dead while on his own pilgrimage to sainthood could be no other than John Paul II. He is the only Pope since 1917 whose ministry so closely matches the details of this vision. John Paul has said as much and Sister Lucia agreed that the one Pope depicted in the third message is John Paul II[54]. She further agreed with John Paul's interpretation[55] that "it was a mother's hand that guided the bullet's path" and "in his throes the Pope halted at the threshold of death" is correct. She added for the sake of clarification, that the vision was not for her to interpret but for the Holy Father. The halting step is also indicated in John Paul's gesture just moments before Agca fired the gun. It has been said that John Paul stopped to kiss and bless a rosary. Lastly the halting step indicates the wisdom of one who considers his actions before performing them.

In the dream when the Pope falls this is much like the halting step of the Pope in the vision. For but a moment the Pope's hands are off the wheel as he is helped up.

Souls of Corpses

The corpses represent those who have separated themselves from God. This is the precursor to eternal death, the culture of death John Paul II warned us of. The culture of death leads to eternal death and permanent separation from God. These corpses do not necessarily represent eternal death but the shadow of it, because they are still able to benefit from the prayers of the faithful through the

---

[54] Conversation With Sister Maria Lucia Of Jesus And The Immaculate Heart, Vatican Website:
http://www.vatican.va/roman_curia/congregations/cfaith/documents/rc_con_cfaith_doc_20000626_message-fatima_en.html
[55] *Meditation with the Italian Bishops from the Policlinico Gemelli, Insegnamenti*, vol XVII/1, 1994, p. 1061

communion of saints, as in purgatory. As a dead body turns cold this may also mean lukewarm Christians.

Martyred at the Foot of the Cross

The fact that the cross is at the top of a mountain shows how great the journey is to sainthood, and equates the climb with that of Jesus' climb up Calvary. As André Frossard remarked to a Parisian newspaper, "This isn't a Pope from Poland; this is a Pope from Galilee." By the time this Pope in the vision reaches the cross he is on his knees from exhaustion or is in worship, or both. Two questions come to mind. How can this Pope be John Paul II who survived an attempted assignation when in the vision he is killed? How can it be John Paul II when in the vision the Pope is shot with bullets and arrows but John Paul II was only shot with bullets? The answer rests in this, that so far we have not taken any of these images to be literal but have applied their symbol to people and events. When we say that John Paul II is that Pope we are not being literal. Rather we are saying that one man personifies this type of Pope more than any other. The problem is not with the answer so much as it is with the question. We ought to ask this differently. We ought to ask, what does death at the hands of soldiers who fire bullets and arrows represent? Let us resist the temptation to say that this means the entire papacy will end in martyrdom. Rather, since the Pope represents all Popes, his death can only represent the faithfulness with which they have committed themselves as His vicar. They die to themselves in order to become most like Christ. The Pope in our modern times that most resembles this archetype is unquestionably John Paul II. That is what we mean when we say this Pope is John Paul II. The bishops and religious, men and women who follow the Pope in the vision and are also martyred must then represent the faithful church following the same path in imitation of Christ.

Likewise, the Pope in the dream falls twice, which implies repeated strikes and injury like the barrage of arrows that strikes the Pope of the vision. And the repeat falls are like those that Jesus endured on the way of the cross.

Soldiers

Figuratively, these are an organized group of men. Though it was one man, Mehmet Ali Agca who shot John Paul II, it has long been suspected by many that Communist groups had contracted him. In March of 2006 the Italian Parliament released a report that the Soviet Military was "beyond any reasonable doubt" responsible for the shooting. Here in this vision heaven may be divulging the culprits as soldiers, members of the military. Another aspect of this image is that they are plural denoting an organized conspiracy, yet conforming to duty. The soldiers may also be equated with the Roman guard who put Jesus to death. Or they may represent sinners whose blasphemies injure the Lord.

In the dream the enemy ships and their crews are not expressly referred to as soldiers, yet is fitting to consider them so since it is a war that is described.

Bullets and Arrows

Bullets are the modern form of arrows. They are those devices, which pierce the flesh, the body of Christ (and thus the Church). At this point in the vision, the body of Christ, the Church is being persecuted. The ammunition may represent blasphemies or actual torture. We should recognize that the tortures inflicted upon this Pope are the same as those inflicted upon the subsequent martyrs.

What sense is being conveyed here is that this Pope is a martyr for the faith. Whatever he suffers, he suffers for Christ and His Church, as do the other martyrs.

The compiled version of the dream in the Biographical Memoirs of John Bosco describes the Pope as falling during a skirmish of hand-to-hand combat. In other texts written by eyewitnesses the Pope falls as a result of the blows the ship takes when the enemies ram her. This latter version fits with the Fatima vision since, as we have seen in a previous chapter, the act of the ramming ships of the dream is a type of piercing just the way the arrows are in the vision. The ramming prows of the ships in the dream are even described as arrows.

The bullets and arrows are the onslaught of the enemy. They are projectiles aimed at targets for the purpose of destruction. In this sense even words spoken or printed can be weapons since they can be aimed and projected at others in an attempt to destroy. We saw this point illustrated in the dream clearly in the chapter *Books, Seas and Storms.*

Ranks and Positions
These are people from all walks of life. This shows the universality and equality of the Church.

Angels Beneath the Two Arms of the Cross
The angels are positioned beneath the cross, showing they are allied with the redemptive plan of God.

Crystal Aspersorium
Ordinarily used for Holy Water, the aspersorium represents baptism. Since the angels gather the blood of the martyrs and sprinkle the remnant pilgrims, it demon-

strates the purity of their lives. In this image baptism is associated with the blood of the martyrs.

Blood of the Martyrs

The blood is shown to be the sign of a kind of baptism for the faithful. It is seen atoning for sins by assisting the faithful on their journey. All of this is done on the path to the cross indicating the cooperation of the martyrs, the pilgrims and the angels. This is also a demonstration of the communion of saints.

The 200 Day March

There is a theory that another of Don Bosco's prophecies explains the Dream of the Great Ship and shares even more similarities with the Third Secret of Fatima. This prophecy known as the Two-Hundred-Day March, also describes a city in ruins, the sun shining brightly, a storm and the intercessory role of our Blessed Mother. However it does not point to John Paul II but Pius IX. You will find the prophecy and possible interpretations in the Appendix: "Resources". It deserves mention here because this information can be found on the Internet and may cause some confusion if not properly addressed. Suffice it to say presently, that several of the symbols in the Two-Hundred-Day March solidly point to the Pope who reigned at the time of the prophecy and not a future Pope or especially not John Paul II.

Weaving a Tapestry

Just as in the Dream of the Great Ship, the Third Secret of Fatima has a Pope who is martyred in battle while on a pilgrimage. In the case of the dream, the Pope is single-mindedly and with all his strength headed for the pillars of Mary and Jesus in the Eucharist. In the case of the Fatima vision the Pope is struggling with halting step uphill to the cross. Both Popes are struck down and neither instance matches perfectly with last century's events. This can be explained by either the symbolic or conditional nature of the vision and dream images. They may represent events the way they would unfold without Mary's intersession and the conversion of hearts. As man freely gives his heart to God, just as through His grace did Mary, humanity cooperates to overcome the evil it has done.

We know for a fact that the Pope in the third Fatima secret is John Paul II. He has said as much himself. The similarities between this Fatima message and the Dream of the Great Ship are reason enough for anyone who wants to agree that the Pope of the dream, who is struck and falls most closely resembles John Paul II over any other modern Pope. Moreover, the vision and the dream both demonstrate that Mary's role in the history of salvation is ongoing. Her work was not completed at the Nativity. As her Son lives, she still works to impart His graces to us.

Most remarkable about this connection between the Third Secret of Fatima and the Dream of the Two Columns is that the dream preceded the vision by fifty-five years and was known to the public during the time that the secret was concealed. Yet who could have imagined that what Saint John Bosco had told in the form of a dream would recur in the form of a vision to three young children? At the time that the Third Secret was safeguarded, who could see the connection? So yes the vision was a secret but not really because Mary's love and intersession is a constant like a foundational thread around which every other thread is weaved in the tapestry that is the Church.

Remedy for the Snake's Bite

The Third Secret of Fatima and Don Bosco's Dream of the Great Ship share the same basic message, that in this time of great strife our devotion to the Eucharist and Mary will secure peace. Mary asks for our devotion to the Eucharist in her request for the first five Saturdays. She said that we should make confession, receive communion and pray the Rosary. By doing this she emphasizes Jesus' holiness. She is pointing out that we should be properly disposed to receive Him as the Eucharist, and that confession appropriately prepares us. She is also saying that we should keep her company by remaining in meditation on the mysteries of Christ's life. Since she stood by Jesus throughout all His ministry and trials, indeed throughout all His life, wherever we find Jesus in these mysteries we also encounter Mary.

This devotion is to be practiced during the first Saturdays[56] of five consecutive months. The prescription for this devotion is outlined in four steps to be carried out on each of the five Saturdays:

1. Make a good Confession
2. Receive Communion
3. Recite Five decades of the Rosary
4. Meditate on fifteen mysteries of the Rosary for fifteen minutes with intention on making reparation to Mary

The dream, too promises that if we place our faith and trust in Jesus as the Eucharist of the Holy Mass we will be safe even amid storms and war. In this respect, the pillar

---

[56] This devotion is sometimes misunderstood to have the requirement of being fulfilled in the first five months of the year, however Our Holy Mother did not express it that way. The only two requirements concerning Saturdays are that they be the first Saturday of the month and that they be five consecutive months.

with the Eucharist is much like the pole with the bronze serpent[57] that Moses was instructed to rise in the desert when the Israelites were besieged by a plague of poisonous snakes. All those who looked at the image were saved. This is the main point of both Fatima and the dream of the two columns. About overcoming the conflict prophesied in the dream Saint John Bosco is recorded to have said, "Only two means can save us amid such turmoil: devotion to Mary Most Holy. Frequent communion, using every means and doing our best to venerate it and have it venerated by everyone everywhere." The Fatima devotion of the first five Saturdays is perhaps the closest answer to Don Bosco's plea because the Fatima devotion unites the Eucharist with the Rosary just like the two pillars in the dream stand together.

What about the timing? Since many of the prophecies illustrated in both the Fatima visions and the dream have come to pass is there still time to respond? Perhaps some of these prophesies came to pass later than perfectly willed, and thus with painful consequences for the Pope and the world, yet the days encompassed in the Fatima visions and also in the Dream of the Great Ship are not complete. They are approaching fulfillment in their allotted number, and the time is still ripe for prayer. It is surely not too late. Remember that in the parable of the Laborers in the Vineyard (Mathew 20) the lord of the vineyard paid the eleventh hour workers the same wage as those who had toiled all day. This is the kind of justice Jesus has in mind for us. The tenth or eleventh hour may be upon us but it is not to late to start working in the field, for our master wills that the harvest should reap in as many as possible.

---

[57] Numbers 21:1-9

PILLARS AND A GREAT PEACE

"Inner peace comes from knowing one is loved by God and from the desire to respond to His love." ~ John Paul II[58]

Two Pillars

John Bosco's biographer Fr. Lemoyne titled the dream *The Two Columns* presumably because the columns of the Eucharist and Mary are the reason Bosco told of the story in the first place. He wanted the boys in the oratory to consider if they were devoted and could withstand the siege. That provokes the question in what way do these pillars help us? At first inspection, the Eucharist and Mary do not seem to be depicted actively doing much. More active help comes from the favorable wind, which is the Holy Spirit. Yet on closer inspection we see their more active role. Since, the source of this favorable wind is the two columns, we could imagine that the Holy Spirit is sent forth by the intersession of Mary and by Christ. The height and size of the Host and Mary provide a stable focal point. Their mere presence assists like beacons and attaching to them brings placidity much the same way that Jesus calmed the storm after the disciples roused Him from sleep (Matt 8:23-2). This is the type of reliance that Saint Bosco wants us to have upon these two pillars of faith. He wanted the boys in the oratory, and subsequently us, to turn to the Eucharist and Mary and plea for mercy and grace for ourselves and others.

---

[58] Message Of His Holiness Pope John Paul II For The Xxviii World Day Of Peace, Women: Teachers Of Peace, 1 January 1995

There are two pillars because two is the number of witness. Both Adam and Eve participated in the original sin. Both the cities of Sodom and Gomorrah were punished for their corruption. John prepared the way for Jesus. Both the Father and the Holy Spirit testify that Jesus is the Christ and the Son of God. In Revelation (chapter 13) two beasts worship the dragon. One comes up from the water, the other from the land. Also in Revelation (chapter 11) there are two witnesses who prophesy and are endowed with great power. Here in the dream there are two columns to testify to the way that brings peace.

Salus Credentium

The Eucharist has many titles and names such as, Blessed Sacrament, Sacrifice of the Mass, Lamb of God, Sacrament of Love, Holy Communion, etc. Each of them highlights a particular facet or dimension over the others. The term Salus Credentium is no different. It means salvation of believers and emphasizes the grace communicated to those who believe. What constitutes a believer? What must one believe in order to receive this salvation? Is it enough to believe that Jesus is the Christ and the Son of God? Indeed no one can confess this except by the Holy Spirit. Yet there is something more required of us if we would partake of eternal life. In John chapter six Jesus explains, "[H]e who believes has eternal life. I am the bread of life... he who eats my flesh and drinks my blood has eternal life, and I will raise him up at the last day. For my flesh is food indeed, and my blood is drink indeed." In this teaching Jesus is not saying believe that He is the Son of God and you'll be saved. Instead, what Jesus fully expects His disciples to believe is that His actual flesh and blood are life giving and that we have to eat and drink Him in order to be raised to eternal life. As a result of this teaching, many disciples returned to their former way of life and no longer accompanied him. Jesus did not stop them from leaving which is affirmation to us that there was no misunderstanding. The disciples truly comprehended the meaning and Jesus tested the twelve he had chosen by asking, "Do you also wish to go away?" Then Peter answered, "Lord, to whom shall we go? You have the words of eternal life; and we have believed, and have come to know, that you are the Holy One of God." Here we see that those who truly believe that Jesus is the Son of God must believe His every word including and especially regarding His flesh and blood.

That requirement to eat and drink His flesh and blood must also remain for those who would later become His disciples. That means there would have to be a way for Jesus to make Himself truly bodily present throughout history even though He ascended to Heaven. This He did when instituting the Eucharist in the upper room on Passover and in conjunction with His complete self-sacrifice throughout His passion, death and resurrection. Luke explains this in chapter twenty-two.

And he took bread, and when he had given thanks he broke it and gave it to them, saying, "This is my body which is given for you. Do this in remembrance of me." And likewise the cup after supper, saying, "This cup which is poured out for you is the new covenant in my blood. ~ Luke 22:19-20

And Paul explains to the Corinthians:

For as often as you eat this bread and drink the cup, you proclaim the Lord's death until he comes. ~ 1 Cor 11:26

The celebration of the Eucharist is not just a one-time memorial or an occasional reenactment but a continual participation in the Lord's death and resurrection. The Eucharist is the evidence and substance of God's love such that in receiving and adoring this sacrament we commune with His love. The Eucharist makes us sharers in the divine life and in this way the Eucharist is the salvation of believers. To moor ourselves to the pillar of the Eucharist is to tie ourselves to this creed. When we settle this in our hearts, our hearts can then be at rest. Saint Augustine explains that only the Lord can satisfy man's heart, "for Thou hast formed us for Thyself [oh Lord], and our hearts are restless till they find rest in Thee."[59] Such is the way by which the Eucharist, source and summit of our faith, brings peace.

Auxilium Christianorum

Mary too has many names and titles such as, Mary Full of Grace, Immaculate Conception, Mother of God, Queen of Heaven, Seat of Wisdom, Ark of the Covenant, the New Eve, Gentle Woman, and countless titles of ladyship. Each of her names expresses one way in which she intercedes for us. Auxilium Christianorum means Help of Christians and appears to be a very general term but is actually making a precise point. Mary helps those who believe in her son Jesus by sharing graces, which she has been given. These graces stem from the same singular grace of her Immaculate Conception.

Eight years prior to the Dream of the Two Columns Pope Pius IX pronounced the Immaculate Conception of Mary as dogma saying, "in the first instance of her

---

[59] *Confessions of Saint Augustine*, Book One, Verse 2

conception, by a singular privilege and grace granted by God, in view of the merits of Jesus Christ, the Savior of the human race, was preserved exempt from all stain of original sin.[60]" This exclamation came at the start of a new devotion that began in 1832. Saint Catherine Laboure' had a vision of The Immaculate Virgin Mary who charged her with the mission to mint a medal with an image on both sides. The front side of the medal bears the image of the Immaculate Virgin Mary and the phrase "O Mary, conceived without sin, pray for us who have recourse to thee". In this image dazzling rays of light are pictured emanating from her hands. These rays of light represent the graces that Mary wishes to give to us if we will only ask her for them. The backside of the medal depicts twelve stars, representing the apostles, the first members of the church. These stars are surrounding the letter M, which stands for Mary. In this way the message on the backside of the medal ensures us that Mary is especially the help of the first Christians. Mary is also the help of anyone who would become a disciple because Christianity is built on a foundation of Jesus and the disciples (Rev 21:14). This is one way in which to see Mary as the help of Christians.

By looking at other biblical references of the set of twelve stars we can gain deeper understanding of their meaning. In Revelation chapter twelve verse one, the woman who appears in heaven as a sign is pictured with a crown of twelve stars. By traditional interpretation this woman is understood to be both the Church and the mother of the Church, Mary[61]. Another place in the Bible that we see twelve stars is in Genesis (chapter 37) in the

---

[60] Pius IX, *Ineffabilis Deus* 1854
[61] Saints Ambrose, Ephrem, Augustine

story of Jacob's favored son Joseph. Joseph has a dream that the sun, the moon and eleven stars bow down to him. The eleven stars represent Joseph's brothers and his star makes up the set of twelve. From this we can see that the number twelve represents divine government, since God ultimately raised Joseph to be a lord second only to Pharaoh. This relationship expresses something about the divine order of things since it was God who raised Joseph to this station where his brother's, even his mother and father are subject to him. In the same way that God had favored Joseph to raise him as second in command so God favored Mary. Yet to Mary the complete set of twelve stars are uniquely given and she is pictured clothed with the sun and with child. Thus signifying three things. One; it was a singular grace by the unique image of the full set of twelve stars. Two; it was the fullness of grace signified by the image of the sun which is the greatest light to the earth. Three; this grace was for the purpose of bringing Jesus Christ into the world, who is the Salvation of Believers. Thus Mary assists in the salvific plan. According to the imagery in Revelation hers is a crown signifying that she is Queen of Heaven by grace.

By singular I mean both one of a kind and once, or in one instance, such that it is complete. In fact, this grace eternally enjoins her with Jesus Christ in a mysterious way and encompasses all four of the Marian dogmas[62] and the doctrine of her coronation as well. Traditionally, as evidenced in the Holy Rosary, the Coronation follows Mary's Assumption into heaven. This would seem as though she is crowned when she is welcomed fully into

---

[62] Apostolic Constitution Of Pope Pius Xii, *Munificentissimus Deus*, Defining The Dogma Of The Assumption, November 1, 1950, section 40

heaven. Yet doctrine explains that Mary is Queen because she is the Mother of Jesus[63] and because of her cooperation in the redemptive plan. Anticipating that she would bear Christ, God gave Mary all grace, which must cover all the dogmas and doctrines that the Church presently teaches about her, including her queenship. This grace elevated her to be the new Eve[64], a role that encompasses governance of all creation. This is evident even at the Annunciation (Lk 1:28) when the angel Gabriel greets Mary, "Hail, full of grace! [65]" The salutation "Hail" is not one given commonly. It is one reserved for royalty. Elizabeth also calls Mary the "mother of my Lord" (Lk 1:43) saying "And why is this granted me, that the mother of my Lord should come to me?" She holds Mary in high regard as in royalty. This status among mankind and angels is one grace that she received from the very moment of her coming into being[66]. The fathers of the Church regarded Mary as "that Queen who, abounding in delights and leaning on her Beloved, came forth from the mouth of the Most High, entirely perfect, beautiful, most dear to God and never stained with the least blemish.[67]" It is clear that the Church's understanding of the favor bestowed on Mary by God is that it is complete grace in view of the full redemptive work of Christ. Accordingly the event that the faithful honor in the Holy Rosary as the Coronation is the glorious fulfillment or the fruition of the same grace that first occurs in earthly time at Mary's Immaculate Conception.

---

[63] *AD CAELI REGINAM*, Encyclical Of Pope Pius Xii On Proclaiming The Queenship Of Mary, October 11, 1954

[64] Irenaeus, book V, chapter XIX, section 1.

[65] Saint. Jerome translated Hebrew and Greek texts into Latin Vulgate. These Latin texts would later be translated into English as the Duey Rheims, which is the version here referenced.

[66] Pius IX, *Ineffabilis Deus* 1854

[67] Ibid

So, Mary has the station of queen from her beginning but she is crowned upon entering heaven body and soul.

According to Rev. 12:1 she is crowned with the twelve stars even before she has given birth to Jesus. In fact, when she first appears as a sign in heaven she is already clothed with the sun, which is the greatest light to the earth and so represents the greatest grace. She is not given a white robe like the martyrs, but is from her first mention clothed in light, which reveals to us that this grace coincides with her coming into being. This seems to be an implication that she was conceived without sin and that this is a sign in heaven. What does the sign signify? It signifies that this woman is the pinnacle of old and new Israel. She is the woman whose son chooses a new Israel, with the twelve disciples as new sons. These are some points among others expressed by the images in the book of Revelation when Mary appears in heaven already crowned.

The grace that Mary received is a manifestation of God's love for all people. Mary received this love in full as grace for all men and thus assists all her children to know, love and serve God[68]. At the foot of the cross Jesus says that Mary is to be a Mother to the disciple John and he is to be her son (Jn 19:25-27). The Church teaches that this means Mary is the mother of all disciples and all people. One moment when Mary's love is our example is when visiting her cousin Elizabeth. In a canticle she says that her soul magnifies the Lord. The love in her heart and the grace in her soul are so great that they increase God's glory. Then at the wedding feast in Cana her last recorded words in the Bible direct others to do whatever Jesus says. This

---

[68] *Lumen Gentium* 61-62

may be why so much of the Church's Marian artwork depicts her either holding the child Jesus or directing us to Him.

With all of this to be said about Mary one would tend to think that it would be the pillar with Mary on it to which we should first moor. Especially since she would point the way to Jesus. Yet in every version of the dream it is the pillar of the Eucharist to which the ship is first moored. This is rightly so because the grace which Mary received was given "in view of the merits of Christ". In other words the merit of the saving work of Christ, though not yet fulfilled on earth, preceded Mary by a special gift from God. And of course, Christ being the eternal son, always was and so He precedes Mary. Another reason why the ship is moored to the Eucharist before Mary rests in the fact that her statue only represents her presence whereas Jesus is truly present in the actual Eucharist. In this dream of Don Bosco's Mary is represented whereas Christ is present. The difference between these two pillars is much like the difference between a sacramental and a sacrament.

There is also a reason why the pillar with the Eucharist on it is taller. In dreams order denotes primacy while size denotes importance. The columns are not of equal stature for the simple fact that what they uphold is not coequal. Jesus is God incarnate, sharing fully in God's power and being from all eternity. Mary is a created being of God whom He filled with grace. So, Mary is a cooperator in grace to the fullest. She gave her fiat, her yes, to cooperate with God for our sake not just during pregnancy and birthing, but like any good mother, for the entire life of her child. Since her child is eternal she continues uninterrupted in giving her consent and in so doing continues to bring us the gifts of eternal salvation[69]. In this way, through continued, uninterrupted and completely free cooperation with the redemptive plan, Mary too assists in bringing about peace.

Putting an End to the End Times Theory

Let us finally turn our attention to dispelling the myth that this dream and particularly these images of war and peace have anything to do with end times. The perplexing subject of end times has been a source of fascination and entertainment for many and this dream does have a few cultic interpretations. A quick search of the Internet will produce ample proof. What is so often ignored among these interpretations is the responsibility associated with the kind of trust that God and John Bosco must have invested in each other. So although John Bosco may not have initially intended the good night talk for external consumption beyond the confines of the oratory, (whether in distance or in time) it is perhaps by divine providence that the faithful and even the secular world have received it. What will we do with it? Will we invest the same kind of trust in God or will we treat it like entertainment taking from it what suits our fancy? Or will we see it in its context as given?

To assist us in viewing the dream of the Great Ship in context we will use a paradigm. As in the past chapters, Mark 7:25-30 will continue to be that requisite paradigm.

---

[69] CCC 969 "This motherhood of Mary in the order of grace continues uninterruptedly from the consent which she loyally gave at the Annunciation and which she sustained without wavering beneath the cross, until the eternal fulfillment of all the elect. Taken up to heaven she did not lay aside this saving office but by her manifold intercession continues to bring us the gifts of eternal salvation. . . . Therefore the Blessed Virgin is invoked in the Church under the titles of Advocate, Helper, Benefactress, and Mediatrix."

In this case it will be our caution not to misapply the symbols. A wrong application in the case of the Syrophoenician women would be to say that dog equals pet, children equal Romans, food equals charity and table equals government. With this kind of interpretation one could justify the idea that it is the duty of the master and the children to feed the pet or stray dogs. In a sense it would be saying that the master and the children have been negligent. This interpretation ignores the contextual analysis that tells us that Jesus and the children He is speaking about are Hebrew. Since Jesus and the children of the story are not Roman this interpretation falls apart. That kind of logic is not historically oriented and also lacks the kind of humility we would expect to find in the true meaning of Jesus' words. The same thing can happen when interpreting Don Bosco's dream, particularly in the context of end times.

So we should ask what images and symbols there are in the dream that provide context. Of course, there are the two Vatican Councils amidst the storm and the Pope who dies. But is there any room for interpreting the storms as cataclysmic precursors to the end of ages? Now let us play the advocate for a moment and ask if the calm over the water is possibly the peace that comes at the consummation of all things? Isn't it fair to take John Bosco's words, "the enemy ships are the persecutions in store for the Church. What has happened up to now is almost nothing," as meaning a persecution yet to come? And isn't it reasonable to say that since the Church will undergo a trial prior to Christ's second coming (CCC 675[70]) which could

---

[70] Before Christ's second coming the Church must pass through a final trial that will shake the faith of many believers. The persecution that accompanies her pilgrimage on earth will unveil the "mystery of iniquity" in the form of a religious deception offering men an apparent solution to their problems at the

be accomplished at any moment, (CCC 673[71]) and that the antichrist's deception has already taken shape in the world (CCC 676[72]), that the dream of the two pillars might be pointing toward it? Shouldn't we be fair in considering it a possibility that is within the boundaries set by magisterial authority and that the faithful are free to believe it? Besides, lasting peace can only exist when Christ returns. The final judgment will see to that, right?

It is a well-formed set of questions but the images of the dream give it no credence. There are essential images expressed in these quotes of the Catechism, which are absolutely necessary if their application is to be worthily applied to the dream yet they are missing from the dream imagery. For instance, who in the dream is the Antichrist? Are the enemies collectively the Antichrist? And where is the apparent solution to man's problems at the price of apostasy? Is it in the books that the enemy uses as weapons? Maybe, but the books have much too small of a role to be depicting an apostasy that would be so great as to deceive even the elect if it were possible. In the absence of these themes it is just not reasonable to consider the dream an end-times prophesy.

---

price of apostasy from the truth. The supreme religious deception is that of the Antichrist, a pseudo-messianism by which man glorifies himself in place of God and of his Messiah come in the flesh

[71] Since the Ascension Christ's coming in glory has been imminent, even though "it is not for you to know times or seasons which the Father has fixed by his own authority." This eschatological coming could be accomplished at any moment, even if both it and the final trial that will precede it are "delayed"

[72] The Antichrist's deception already begins to take shape in the world every time the claim is made to realize within history that messianic hope which can only be realized beyond history through the eschatological judgment. The Church has rejected even modified forms of this falsification of the kingdom to come under the name of millenarianism, especially the "intrinsically perverse" political form of a secular messianism

There is nothing unique about the dream, which is placed in our age, that points to the end of times. In fact the opposite is true. There is a unique occurrence at the end of the dream, which actually points to a continuation. The ship is docked between two columns in the middle of the ocean, where there is no land in sight. What successful voyage ends in the middle of the ocean? This is no final destination, for the ultimate destination of the Church is the Father. If this were the end we would expect to see Zion like a great mountain or a city on a hill where God and man dwell together in perfect reconciliation. These images simply aren't here nor are they implied. Nor could we know the moment of the end factually. Instead, what we can know is what season we are in presently.

For Clarity sake, let us acknowledge that precise moments, like the day and hour of Christ's return are for the Father alone to know (Mat 24:36), yet it is not wrong to know that there are times and seasons, or even to know which is the present season. True, Jesus told His disciples not to concern themselves about knowing the seasons (Acts 1: 6-8[73], Mark 13:32-33[74]), yet he also rebuked the Pharisees and Sadducees for not knowing them (Mat 16:1). Jesus did this because the Pharisees and Sadducees refused to acknowledge His miracles as messianic signs. Which means they did not recognize Him as the hope of Israel because they chose to ignore the signs that the prophets had foretold about the time of Christ's arrival.

---

[73] When they had gathered together they asked him, "Lord, are you at this time going to restore the kingdom to Israel?" He answered them, "It is not for you to know the times or seasons that the Father has established by his own authority. But you will receive power when the Holy Spirit comes upon you, and you will be my witnesses in Jerusalem, throughout Judea and Samaria, and to the ends of the earth."

[74] "But of that day or hour, no one knows, neither the angels in heaven, nor the Son, but only the Father. Be watchful! Be alert! You do not know when the time will come.

So on the one hand we are not to be overly concerned about the ages to come but on the other hand we are to concern ourselves with our present age. It is a sufficient burden then, for this present age and for our intellects and faith that we should discern that Jesus is the Messiah, the Son of God. In other words, it is enough that we concern ourselves over Christ's first coming and not be obsessed about His second coming; trying to predict when exactly it will be. Certainly, we look and pray for the resurrection and the glorious day of His return. This is part of the vigilance we keep in joyful hope especially when we celebrate the Holy Mass, because it is the proper way and context in which to expect His return. So it is right to consider the signs and learn the seasons in their proper context. In the case of the dream the context is the most Holy Eucharistic as evidenced by the gigantic pillar with the host on it. The Eucharist is the largest thing in this vast panorama because it is the apex, the source and summit of our faith[75]. As the sign on the pillar says, it is the Salvation of Christians.

The calm water at the end of the dream is an image describing the power of the Eucharist that puts the world at rest. In previous chapters we have seen how the tempests in the dream are times of cultural upheaval and war. What then is the placid water at the end of this saga but peace where the world was once restless? A similar image is found three times in the book of Revelation. First in chapter 4 verses 5 and 6 the throne of God is described as having seven flaming torches and a sea of glass before it. Then in chapter 7 verse 9 a great multitude is seen dressed in white and holding palm branches. Finally, in chapter 15 verse 2 the martyred are also dressed in white

---

[75] *Lumen Gentium*, No 11, CCC 1324

robes and are standing on a sea of glass mixed with fire. Here the Triumphant Church is pictured standing on water the way Jesus walked on it. In this context, the sea must represent more than the condition of world affairs. It must represent judgment and death, for those living in Christ have conquered it. Also, it was the means by which the world was judged except for Noah and those on the ark. It was the means by which Pharaoh's army was destroyed while Moses and the Israelites passed through it. In both the Flood and the Exodus, the mercy and grace of God extended to man a means of salvation. In Revelation chapter five the Lamb who was slain and is worthy to open the scroll is our salvation. In Revelation chapter seven those martyrs who stand on the lake of glass have been cleansed by the blood of the lamb. So in Revelation we see a relationship between the Lamb and the still water. We see that same relationship in the dream of the great ship between the Eucharist and the still water. In this way both the dream and Revelation illustrate the power of the Eucharistic sacrifice to overcome sin and bring peace.

The similarities and differences between the two images of placid waters show us that they are about the same event, one that unites Heaven and Earth. This can only be the Holy Mass. In the dream the Church depicted is the Church Militant. We know this in several ways. The ship of the Church is engaged in war, which means she is struggling against sin and temptation. It takes place on Earth, and the ship they are on is the bark of Peter with a Pope at the helm. In these chapters of Revelation there is no war to identify with the Church Militant. Instead the martyrs stand directly on the water showing that they have conquered death and are thus belonging to the Church Triumphant. The placid waters of the dream are near the Eucharist while the placid waters of Revelation are in front of the throne[76]. The two pillars in the dream assist the pilgrims on the ship to conquer the battle against sin and the temptations of the world the flesh and the devil. In contrast, the lamp stands of Revelation along with their fire that represents judgment are signs that these temptations have been overcome.

Clearly this imagery is not the devastating apocalypse so popularly promoted today. Rather, this imagery is that of the Mass, the sacrament that joins Heaven and Earth through the continuing sacrifice of Christ. So the real problem with seeing end times in Don Bosco's dream is not in relating it to Revelation but in misunderstanding these parts of Revelation to begin with.

Great Peace

We have dealt enough with Judgment and end times so Let us ask questions about the great peace seen in the placid waters of the dream and which comes from the Eucharist. Is it only peace for the Church or is it peace for the world? Is it the same peace that Mary promised at Fatima? Could that peace, worldly or spiritual, encompass a revival of Pentecost and a new springtime in the Church? Let us look at the seasons of the ages, also referred to as the times, and see how peace fits in.

---

[76] One could say that the monstrance or the pillar is the throne for the Eucharist, which being Jesus, is God. In this way there is an earthly parallel to heavenly things as described in the Our Father prayer, "Thy kingdom come one Earth as it is in Heaven."

<u>A Time for Peace</u>
The first chapter of Ecclesiastes describes 14 pairs of times, each with a thesis and corresponding antithesis. These are the times appointed by God:

a time to be born, and a time to die;
a time to plant, and a time to pluck up what is planted;

a time to kill, and a time to heal;
a time to break down, and a time to build up;

a time to weep, and a time to laugh
a time to mourn, and a time to dance;

a time to cast away stones, and a time to gather stones together;
a time to embrace, and a time to refrain from embracing

a time to seek, and a time to lose
a time to keep, and a time to cast away;

a time to rend, and a time to sew
a time to keep silence, and a time to speak;

a time to love, and a time to hate;
a time for war, and a time for peace.

Notice that it begins with the genesis of man and the fact of his mortality, a time to be born and a time to die. And associated with that is the time to plant and reap. That is our commission and punishment, to till the ground by the sweat of our brow. It ends with the time of peace just as in the Dream of the Great Ship and in Fatima. In order to understand the seasons as appointed times, let's look closer at the literary structure. The fact that there are 14 pairs (28 total times) or 4 sets of 7 is significant. Four is the number pertaining to the earth (four winds, four horsemen, four corners of the earth etc.) Seven is the number of perfection (six days to create the Earth and a seventh for Sabbath rest, six years to till the earth and a seventh for Sabbath rest, perfect forgiveness is 70 times 7 times, 7 deadly sins, 7 sacraments, etc). This shows us that the affairs of man and Church (earthly affairs) have seasons counted out in perfect sevens just like a week. There can be a week of days, a week of years, and a week of millenniums. With this in mind we can draw a parallel between the creation and the death and resurrection of our Lord.

In the creation story, the days which are most elaborated are the sixth and seventh days where the creation and fall of man are described. The sixth day describes in detail the creation of man and the seventh day describes his betrayal of God in the garden, on the day of rest, God's work being accomplished. In the passion of Christ we see Jesus, the new man, in obedience and agony in the garden beginning Thursday night, which in Hebrew calculations is actually Friday, the sixth day. According to Genesis the evening (antithesis) and the morning (thesis) count as the next day:

…And there was evening and there was morning, a sixth day.
~ Genesis 1:31

He spent the rest of Friday in trial, scourging and crucifixion. Saturday, the seventh day, the day of Sabbath rest His body lay in the tomb, His work being accomplished. Early in the morning, on the first day of the new week, Jesus rose.

This same paradigm may be applied to millennial years and the Church. According to Peter, his traditional understanding of Psalm 90 is that a thousand years equals a day to the Lord:

For a thousand years in thy sight are but as yesterday when it is past, or as a watch in the night ~ Psalms 90:4

But do not ignore this one fact, beloved, that with the Lord one day is as a thousand years, and a thousand years as one day.
~ 2 peter 3:8

This fits the paradigm. Four thousand years of Hebraic history plus two thousand years of Christian history complete six days of the week (6000 years = 6 days to God). Christ died on the sixth day, spent the seventh day, which is the Sabbath, in the tomb. He rose on the first day of the new week. So too did His church "die" near the end of the second thousand years of Church history, which is the six thousandth year or sixth day of Salvation History. So the Church is just entering into the age of peace, and Sabbath rest. Just as Jesus and Jonah spent the Sabbath in the belly of the whale[77] so too does the Church follow.

In order to properly chart this you need to keep in mind that the Hebrew calendar and the measure of a day differ from the Gregorian calendar and 24 hr clock that we use today. Ordinarily we begin counting the day at midnight whereas traditionally the Jewish way is to start counting in the evening when the first three stars are visible.

---

[77] "Just as Jonah was in the belly of the whale three days and three nights, so will the Son of Man be in the heart of the earth three days and three nights." ~ Mat 12:40

The Dream of the Great Ship fits into this paradigm at the sixth day and ends at the eve of the seventh day. The ship in the dream represents the Church. The arrow/spear-shaped prow beaks of the enemy ships pierce the great ship, the Church, the body of Christ. This parallels the moment when the centurion pierced the side of Christ and blood and water came forth. This dates the time when the dream is fulfilled as the age of the Church's crucifixion and death on the sixth day of Salvation History. The Catechism of the Catholic Church expresses a parallel between the passion of Christ and His bride.

The Church will enter the glory of the kingdom only through this final Passover, when she will follow her Lord in his death and Resurrection. ~ CCC 677

Does this mean that the Church will end? And what if the Pope in the dream represents the entire papacy rather than a few particular Popes then we must contend with the idea the papacy would somehow die and be restored. That is what death would imply figuratively but is this possible? Can the church or the papacy end? Many a good Catholic knows that Jesus promised the Church would have no end:

"...and he will reign over the house of Jacob for ever; and of his kingdom there will be no end." ~ Lk 1:33

And

"And I tell you, you are Peter, and on this rock I will build my church, and the powers of death shall not prevail against it."
  ~ Mat 16:18

								NEW WEEK
Calendar Week		Sun	Mon	Tue	Wed	Thu	Fri	Sat	Sun
Day / Night									
Biblical		Day 1	Day 2	Day 3	Day 4	Day 5	Day 6	Day 7	Day 1
Creation Week		Light	Sky	Land, Sea, Plants	Sun, Moon, Stars	Sea Creatures, Birds	Land Creature, Man	Sabbath Rest	Salvation History Begins
Passion Week							Agony in the Garden	Crucifixion and Burial	Resurrection
Millennium Week		4000 Years of Hebraic History				2000 Years of Christian History		Christianity Continues (present day)	

© Tim Bartel 2007

So this is a bit of a stumbling block, problematic but answerable. For if the death of the Pope in the dream were meant to express the death of the papacy, then the ensuing election of a new Pope would imply a resurrection of the papacy. But that would mean that every Interregnum is a type of death and resurrection of the Church. Every Interregnum then begins with a Good Friday and ends with an Easter Sunday. John Paul II and Benedict XVI exemplify this archetypal parallel.

In previous chapters we have shown how John Paul II was certainly a man who played out his passion on a world stage as a type of suffering Christ. He carried a cross inwardly for those friends and family that he lost in and around World War II and the cold war and for all oppressed people. In his later years he carried a cross of physical pain with Parkinson's disease. He saw his papacy in relation to the message of Divine Mercy and canonized Sister Faustina who had been its messenger. He did this on the same day that he officiated Divine Mercy Sunday as the second Sunday of Easter. In his address at the Shrine of Divine Mercy 1997 he said, "The message of Divine Mercy has always been dear to me…which in a sense forms the image of this pontificate." Divine Mercy pictures Jesus with two rays emanating from His Heart, one white and one red. The white ray denotes our baptism with the water that purifies and the red denotes His Mercy through the shedding of His blood, which is our life. These two rays issued forth from His side when the centurion pierced it with a spear. This is how John Paul saw his papacy, in the context of the mercy of Jesus Crucified and pierced, in the context of the suffering and dying Christ. John Paul's death even occurred on the vigil of Divine Mercy Sunday. This message couldn't be any clearer. He was single-minded in this like the Pope in the dream who strains every muscle to keep the ship on course. This goal was his passion the way Jesus' goal to suffer and die for our sake was His passion. John Paul's papacy was a Good Friday papacy.

Benedict XVI's life and papacy follows as a Sabbath papacy, one on the vigil of Easter. In an interview with Peter Seewald he explained how he saw his own situation saying, "I am pleased to have been born on the Vigil of Easter, already on the way to Easter but not quite there, for it is still veiled. I find that a very good day, which in some sense hints at my own conception of history and my own situation; on the threshold of Easter but not yet through the door." This is how Benedict sees himself, as one anticipating Christ with joy.

So we can see the whole papacy reflected in the dream of the two columns. We can also see the pattern of death and election of Popes as a type of Triduum, which John Paul II and Benedict XVI in part epitomize. Now, how can the whole of the Church parallel Christ in dying over the Sabbath and rising on the next day without ever ending? In other words is there a way in which the Church can die and yet still be the visible presence of Christ's body on Earth? Yes. Archbishop Fulton Sheen explains it:

"The Church has a Good Friday and an Easter Sunday. It does not proceed on a level. It dies. And then it grows again to a new life. I would say that there is a great death about once every five hundred years. History seems to run in those cycles. In the first cycle of five hundred years there was the fall of Rome.... In the second cycle of five hundred years we had the Muslim invasion and the Eastern Schism. Then the third cycle of five hundred years was the religious revolution [reformation]. Now we are in the fourth cycle of five-hundred years and we are

undergoing a crisis, like to some extent to the others which happened in the same cycle of years[78]."

And:

"I think that this fourth stage we are in now is the end of Christendom. Not the end of Christianity obviously. What do I mean by Christendom? By Christendom I mean the economic, political, social life of a nation as governed by the Gospel ethic. That I believe is dead in the world."

So this is another way of understanding that there are divinely appointed times to be born and to die, to plant and sew. The Church moves through seasons of times dying to herself and rising again like her beloved spouse Jesus Christ. These seasons are expressed not just in Ecclesiastes but also in the laws brought to the people through Moses, in particular the Third Commandment, which is to remember the Sabbath and keep it holy.

Sabbatical & Jubilee Seasons

The five hundred year cycle of trial and death, peace and growth in the Church also matches a timeline comprised of sevens. The sevens are based upon the commandment to remember the Sabbath and keep it holy. The Sabbath day being the seventh day of the week, Saturday, the day the Lord rested after creation.

Sabbatical

According to Levitical rule the land was to be farmed six years and then given a year of rest in the seventh year,

---

[78] Excerpts by Archbishop Fulton Sheen are from a recorded retreat in the 1970's titled Priest as Victim. He gave this talk a number of times. One version is available through Saint Joseph's Communications (www.saintjoe.com) and another through Keep the Faith (www.keepthefaith.org)

known as a sabbatical year. These seven years made up a week of years (each year counting as one day of a week). Just as the Sabbath at the end of the week is holy so too is the Sabbath at the end of a week of years holy. In the Sabbath year the land was to go un-serviced and the crops left un-harvested. The only exception was what could be eaten directly from the field without gathering.

<u>Jubilee</u>

At the end of seven weeks of years (forty-nine years OR seven times seven years) a jubilee year was observed. The jubilee year itself brings the total cycle of years to fifty, which is approximately one generation. In the Jubilee year all debts were forgiven, Hebrew slaves and their wives were freed, and land returned to its owner. This jubilee was observed in addition to the sabbatical year that falls the year prior, such that every forty-ninth and fiftieth year the land is left fallow.

> *"A jubilee shall that fiftieth year be to you; in it you shall neither sow, nor reap what grows of itself, nor gather the grapes from the undressed vines. For it is a jubilee; it shall be holy to you; you shall eat what it yields out of the field. "In this year of jubilee each of you shall return to his property..."*"
> ~ *Leviticus 25:11-13*

The jubilee year was truly a year of remission and universal pardon, a time for celebration. The fundamental governing this remission is that the land belongs to God. It is the deeply rooted Mosaic Law that makes our redemption practical. For the institution of the Jubilee foreshadows Jesus ransoming captive Israel[79]. In *Tertio*

---

[79] According to Luke 3:23 Jesus is a Levite through His step father Joseph. According to Mosaic Law, a Levite does not have to wait till the Jubilee year to

Millennio Adveniente, an apostolic letter dated November 11, 1994 John Paul writes in anticipation of the millennial Jubilee in 2000:

"...for the Church, the jubilee is precisely this 'year of the Lord's favor,' a year of remission of sins and of the punishments due them, a year of reconciliation between disputing parties, a year of manifold conversions and of sacramental and extra-sacramental penance.... Jubilees are celebrated not only in Urbe [of place or time] but also extra Urbem [beyond place and time]."~

And

"With regard to its content, this Great Jubilee will be, in a certain sense, like any other. But at the same time it will be different, greater than any other. For the Church respects the measurements of time: hours, days, years, centuries. She thus goes forward with every individual, helping everyone to realize how each of these measurements of time is imbued with the presence of God and with his saving activity. In this spirit the Church rejoices, gives thanks and asks forgiveness, presenting her petitions to the Lord of history and of human consciences."

Perfect Forgiveness

There is a type of 'jubilee' that man experiences by observing the divine law to forgive. This is because God forgives us as we forgive others. Just how perfect are we to be in practicing this divine law? Peter had the same question:

---

redeem his land. He can redeem it at any time. Thus Jesus could redeem the earth and us, its produce, at any time.

"Then Peter came up and said to him, "Lord, how often shall my brother sin against me, and I forgive him? As many as seven times?" Jesus said to him, "I do not say to you seven times, but seventy times seven."" ~ *Matthew 18:21-22*

Seventy times seven, equals four hundred and ninety years. This is approximately the time that the Israelites spent in chastisement under the rulership of the Meads, Persians and the Babylonians. Only after that time of purgation would the acceptable time of the Lord come, the time of Christ. All of church history can be viewed in terms of these perfect times of forgiveness, or spiritual jubilees. Archbishop Fulton Sheen points out the ages of Church trials since the Death and Resurrection of our Lord:

"In the first five-hundred years the church was concerned with Christological heresies. Everything centered around the historical Christ. How many intellects did he have? How many wills? How many natures? How many persons? This was the great worry of the Church in that first cycle. In the next cycle of five hundred years it was not the historical Christ that was the issue. It was the head of the church. The Holy Father. Because the Eastern Schism broke with him. In the Third cycle of five hundred years, it was not the historical Christ, it was not the head of the Church, it was the body of the Church… Now where are we in this cycle? There are no more heresies concerning Christ except just an incidental one here and there, or the head of the Church or the body of the Church. Today the great concern is the world around us. It is ecological as it were. It is the environment in which the Church lives. It is the world and what is to be our attitude toward it. The Vatican Council for the

first time in the history of the Church discussed the world. That was chapter thirteen.[80]"

So the Church continually dies and rises, much like the sacrifice of the mass, which is not a repeat death and resurrection, but a continual sacrifice and resurrection in which or Lord fills the tabernacle, fills us with Himself.

Sabbath Tabernacle

While Pope Benedict XVI was still known as Cardinal Ratzinger he wrote *Spirit of the Liturgy* in which he explained, "Seven times [Exodus] says, "Moses did as the Lord had commanded him", words that suggest that the seven-day work on the tabernacle replicates the seven-day work on creation. The account of the construction of the tabernacle ends with a kind of vision of the Sabbath. "So Moses finished the work. Then the cloud covered the tent of meeting, and the glory of the LORD filled the tabernacle" (Ex 40:33f.).[81]" So we can see that the creation of the world, the building of the tabernacle, and the institution of the Sabbath all are related in this one purpose; to make the Earth the meeting place of man and God. This is the perfect peace in the dream, the perfect calm at sea when God and man are reconciled. Remembering that this reconciliation occurs only when moored first to the pillar of the Eucharist it becomes evident that this pilgrimage across a tumultuous sea, against enemy attacks, and amid storms and confusion is none other than the Church's journey to discover proper liturgy of the Eucharist.

---

[80] There is no thirteenth chapter in any of the Vatican Documents. He may be referring to item 13 of chapter 1 in *Gaudium et Spes* [Pastoral Constitution On The Church In The Modern World], which deals with the dignity of man through his suffering in the light and knowledge of Christ his redeemer.

[81] Joseph Cardinal Ratzinger, *The Spirit of the Liturgy*, Ignatius Press, 2000, pgs 26, 27

A Biblical Triduum Prayer Vigilance

What part do the people have to play in this journey to perfect liturgy? How do we actualize our role in the preparation of the tabernacle? An answer may be found in the vigilance that Jesus requires of His disciples at the start of His passion in the garden of Gethsemane, "watch and pray that you may not undergo the test" (Mk 14:37).

A story in Tobit describes a three-day period of prayer and purgation in anticipation of the consummation of marriage, which reflects the union of God and man, and in this sense relates to the Liturgy. Tobit was engaged to a woman who had been married seven times. Each time the new husband died while in the bridal chambers[82]. The archangel Raphael explains to Tobit to wait three days after marriage before consummating it, praying during those nights instead. That time of purgation worked and the marriage was blessed and consummated. This Triduum of prayer and vigilance is what the Church and Christ are doing. If we look at the history of the Catholic Church we see that God made a promise, a covenant, which is like an engagement that has lasted two thousand years. During those years that are like days to God, we the bride are being made holy, set apart, as we pray for the day of His return and the consummation of all things. If this analogy is correct, then we ought to watch and pray because it is the proper fulfillment of the Sabbath day. Without this vigilance we fall prey to the devils that seek the ruin of our souls. Either we pray or we are preyed upon. This is just what happened in the garden on the Sabbath. Man failed his great trial of obedience and trust in God, and succumbed to the temptation of the serpent.

---

[82] The Sadducees referenced Tobit when they tested Jesus' knowledge and understanding of scripture. See Luke 20:27-40

Peace of Christ

As part of His discourses at the Last Supper, Jesus gave the disciples His peace, yet what ensued was chaos. Jesus was abandoned, arrested, stood before a mock trial, was condemned, falsely accused before Herod and Pilot, beaten, blasphemed and crucified. Most of the disciples fled, with the exception of John because he was right there at the foot of the cross with Mary, who was a pillar of strength to him. Immediately after Christ's Resurrection and the restoration of the twelve, the newly formed Church of Christians began to be martyred. Also in the Churches inception were heresies, which she vehemently countered. This continued until 313 when Emperor Constantine published the Edict of Milan, which formally tolerated Christianity and established all religion as absolutely independent from state interference. Constantine also ordered that the state pay to restore all property seized during the prior persecution of Diocletian. This edict, which appears to be like a Jubilee, came to be known as The Peace of the Church. Is this the peace that Christ gave finally showing up after three hundred years? Certainly the Church has rest when there is no persecution, but that is not the real cause or definition of peace. At the Celebration of the World Day of Peace January first, 2006, Pope Benedict XVI quoted and paraphrased *Gaudium et Spes* section 78, which explains the proper understanding of peace:

"...peace cannot be reduced to the simple absence of armed conflict, but needs to be understood as ''the fruit of an order which has been planted in human society by its divine Founder'', an order ''which must be brought about by humanity in its thirst for ever more perfect justice'''". ~ Benedict XVI, January 1, 2006

Peace is more than the absence of evil; it is the presence of good. It is the same way with darkness and light and it might be easier to look at it that way. Both darkness[83] and evil have no substance, while both goodness and light[84] do. So evil and darkness are the absence of goodness and light, but goodness and light must be substantively present. Evil and darkness only have meaning relative to goodness and light, while goodness and light have meaning of their own accord. Peace then, is like the day; it may be understood to be the material and substantive presence of goodness and light. This is evident in Revelation where Jesus Himself illuminates the New Jerusalem:

"And in the Spirit he carried me away to a great, high mountain, and showed me the holy city Jerusalem coming down out of heaven from God, having the glory of God, its radiance like a most rare jewel, like a jasper, clear as crystal."
~ *Revelation 21:10-11*

"And the city has no need of sun or moon to shine upon it, for the glory of God is its light, and its lamp is the Lamb."
~ *Revelation 21:23*

His peace as manifested in us then, is that confidence of knowing He has reconciled us with God the Father and that He dwells with and in us (especially, at the Holy Mass). Like Eucharistic Prayer III expresses, 'Lord, may this sacrifice, which has made our peace with you, advance the peace of the world.' We can know with even greater certainty that the peace, which Jesus gives, is not

---

[83] Darkness can only be quantified relative to the absence of light.
[84] Light is made up of particles that behave either independently as particles or corporately in waves.

the same as the peace the world gives. He said so Himself at the Last Supper:

"Peace I leave with you; my peace I give to you; not as the world gives do I give to you. Let not your hearts be troubled, neither let them be afraid." ~ John 14:27

Jesus' example of suffering and His sacrifice grant us peace in our own trials. Let us play the advocate again and ask; if Jesus promised us peace and what materially followed was a bloodbath, should we be concerned about what's coming to us according to the Dream of the Great Ship and Fatima? Even though we are not to be troubled or afraid doesn't this mean that receiving His peace means impending trial? First, His grace is sufficient for us in any age and His grace is our peace. Second, in the dream and the vision the peace described is much more like the calm after the storm. In the case of the dream, that analogy is portrayed practically verbatim.

Peace is a gift bestowed on humanity when we seek it. We must first order ourselves toward the perfect order of God. That is what the ships in the dream are doing when they moor themselves to the giant pillars of the Eucharist and Mary. It is what the post-conciliar Popes have intended by upholding the Novus Ordo Mass. They have strained to keep the Church on course with the renewal of the Liturgy and to bring to fruition what the Council sowed. Both John Paul I and John Paul II in their *Urbi et Orbi* addresses expressed the "unceasing importance[85]" of "Implementing without interruption the legacy left us by the Second Vatican Council.[86]" Most recently Benedict

---

[85] Pope John Paul II, *Urbi et Orbi* address, Oct 17, 1978
[86] Pope John Paul I, *Urbi et Orbi* address, Aug 27 1978

XVI, by his Motu Proprio, *Summorum Pontificum* has not only liberated the Traditionalists to participate in the Latin Mass but has directed the Novus Ordo to be formed after it, such that each of these two forms of the one Roman Rite mutually enriches the other. This small document and accompanying letter is a sure sign of the chain that holds us to the Eucharist and assures us of the type of worship the Council intended for the new order of the Mass. As we begin to realize the true intentions of the Council the new age of peace and the new springtime will manifest.

Since we have established that the season in which we are now living is the season which the Dream of the Great Ship depicts, we know that the calm at the end of it is the beginning of a new age. It is an age of peace. Friday at the moment of Christ's death on the cross has just ended. What comes next is the long Sabbath rest in the tomb. This is the perfect peace that stills the waters of the Earth, and the peace that Mary promised at Fatima. It is a peace the Jesus grants when we devote ourselves to the pillars of Mary through the Rosary and the Eucharist in Liturgy.

The Other Ships

We hope that this new era will slowly show us the fruits of our ecumenical efforts with other religions and nations. These are the ships that stayed at a safe distance, perhaps prudently. This distance can be seen as a theological difference that moves with an ebb and tide. Consider the *Joint Declaration on the Doctrine of Justification*, which has been reached between the Lutheran World Federation and the Catholic Church. Even though this, the reason for the Lutheran split from Rome, is resolved Lutherans still have not rejoined the Catholic Church. That's because in the interim a new point of division has developed. The main point of division is now clearly the Eucharist.

Will governments, institutions, and economic alliances based on flawed philosophies that ignore the dignity of man scuttle themselves into oblivion? That is what the dream predicts by describing the ships of the dream as colliding with one another.

Although we might have a smaller church at first we hope for a record increase in conversions. This has always been the case after cycles of great trial. After the Christological heresies and the fall of Rome in the first five centuries, the Church expanded throughout Europe. After the Muslim Invasion in the latter half of the first millennium came the middle ages and a growth in theology. After the religious revolution (Reformation[87]) came missionary enterprises like the Salesians who saint John Bosco founded after Francis de Sales. In South America, millions of natives were converted through the miraculous image of Guadalupe, which pictures Mary almost identical to the woman of Revelation chapter twelve. We should expect ecumenical relations to flourish in the wake of the great world wars, which were fueled by anti-theological philosophies as mentioned in the previous chapter "Books, Seas and Storms".

"A new missionary age will arise, a new springtime for the Church" ~ John Paul II, homily, May 11, 1991

And

---

[87] The term Reformation is a misnomer. It did not need to be re-formed. The form that Jesus gave to the Church was and is perfect. However, its members needed to conform to the original form. Similarly, much of the post-Vatican II problems could be resolved by conforming to the true spirit of its decrees.

"What these Popes have accomplished during and since the [Second Vatican] Council, in their Magisterium no less than in their pastoral activity, has certainly made a significant contribution to the preparation of that new springtime of Christian life which will be revealed by the Great Jubilee, if Christians are docile to the action of the Holy Spirit." ~ *John Paul II, Tertio Millennio Adveniente, November 11, 1994*

According to, then Cardinal Ratzinger, the youth are the hope of this new springtime:

"This is springtime, if new life in very convinced persons with the joy of the faith... if we have young people really with the joy of the faith and this radiation of this joy of the faith, this will show to the world, even if I can not share it, if I can not convert it in this moment, here is the way to life for tomorrow." ~ *Cardinal Joseph Ratzinger, EWTN interview by Ramon Arroyo, Summer 2003*

Although the dream of the two columns would seem to depict boatloads of people converting to Catholicism, and Pope John Paul II said as much, Pope Benedict XVI looks to the youth to slowly bring about conversions:

"My idea is that the springtime of the Church will not say that we will have, in a near time, masses of conversions, that all people of the world will be converted to Catholicism. This is not the way of God. The essential things in history begin always with small, more convinced communities. The Church begins with the twelve apostles." ~ *Cardinal Joseph Ratzinger, EWTN interview by Ramon Arroyo, Summer 2003*

Indeed, in the dream the great peace begins with the one great ship. Then the others follow. Still the entire nation of Israel was brought out of bondage from Egypt virtually overnight. In Acts 16 the jailer's entire household was saved by his faith and the sacrament of Baptism. At Pentecost three thousand were baptized because of Peter's one speech and the work of the Holy Spirit. Such things are historical and theologically sound. What is missing is our cooperation with the spirit, as John Paul II expressed, there is a contingency before the Spirit rains down on us a new springtime. We must be open to the spirit, which means converting and conforming our lives to Christ through the Eucharist and through Mary.

Conclusion

The message of this dream is simple to see but hard for the world to accept. Stay on board the great ship that is the Church, be single-minded like the Pope who is captain, and moor yourself to the Eucharist and Mary, the two giant pillars of safety amongst a turbulent sea of doubt. With devotion to Christ in the Holy Eucharist and devotion to Mary though the Rosary, calm and peace is more than possible; it's promised.

It may come as a disappointment to some that these signs do not point to an age of the end of all times. Yet it should comfort many more to know that a time of mercy and reconciliation with God and a new springtime is at hand. A doomsday interpretation to these prophecies is easy to promote. It suits a contemporary fad and would probably sell more books. Preaching peace while chaos still dominates the globe is far more challenging, truthful and pertinent. Yet there is a danger here. Some may interpret this as preaching the less than imminent return of Christ, by human standards. Surely the end time events Jesus prophesied during His visible stay on Earth are echoed in our own times and could come to fruition at any moment. I do not mean to say that we can all relax for another thousand years. I am just pointing out that this particular prophecy and that of Fatima both point toward a time of peace; peace in trusting that although we Christians are separate from the world we can never be separated from God's love. I am also pointing out that this peace results directly from devotion to both the Eucharist and Mary and the true reform of the Liturgy of the Mass.

You may notice, as I did, an unintentional theme that developed throughout this book; the theme of the Church following Christ in suffering, especially the piercing of Christ's side. The moment of piercing came up when considering the iron arrow and prow beaks of the enemy ships. It came up when considering John Paul II as the Pope of the dream who is struck and falls. It came up when considering the messages at Fatima, both in Mary's words to the visionaries and in the images of the Third Secret. It also came up earlier in this chapter when considering the timeline of the history of salvation. It was not by my design, for at least until now, I have known no particular devotion to the side-wound of Christ. Yet I see that it means much in relation to the Church and the way we follow after Christ's example. If out of His side came the sacramental signs of blood and water[88], then what is to come from this present moment in salvation history when the spear of scandal pierces the Church? The Church was

---

[88] The Fathers of the Church often meditated on the relationship between Eve's coming forth from the side of Adam as he slept (cf. *Gen* 2:21-23) and the coming forth of the new Eve, the Church, from the open side of Christ sleeping in death: from Christ's pierced side, John recounts, there came forth blood and water (cf. *Jn* 19:34), the symbol of the sacraments. A contemplative gaze "upon him whom they have pierced" (*Jn* 19:37) leads us to reflect on the causal connection between Christ's sacrifice, the Eucharist and the Church. The Church "draws her life from the Eucharist". Since the Eucharist makes present Christ's redeeming sacrifice, we must start by acknowledging, "there is a causal influence of the Eucharist at the Church's very origins". ~ Pope Benedict XVI *Sacramentum Caritatis* Part One paragraph 14

born from the side of Christ. Will she not then be renewed through following in like manner after Him and in celebrating the continuing act of His sacrificial love? The new springtime by this supreme standard will be born out of the Sacrament of love, out of renewed faith in the Holy Eucharist and a conformed[89] Liturgy. This is what the dream foretells when it illustrates the Pope, after being pierced, routing the auxiliary ships and mooring to the pillar with the giant host. The act of mooring the great ship to the pillars does not correspond to a singular document or decree but rather to the common faith in the Eucharist that we are all inspired to rekindle. It is this same faith that invites and invokes the Holy Spirit to "transform the bread into the body of Christ and the wine into the blood of Christ. Whatever the Holy Spirit touches is sanctified and completely transformed.[90]" So come Holy Spirit bring us the springtime that is born out of the sacrifice. Like bread and wine transform us and make us the one body of Christ. Amen.

---

[89] Although Reform is the word that describes the change expressed by the Second Vatican Council, I wish to stress the need for the Mass to be celebrated in accordance with this reform. That is why I have chosen the word conform instead of reform.
[90] Saint Cyril, *Jerusalem Catecheses* Mysteries V, lecture XXIII, 7

- OUT IN THE DEEP -

This bonus section covers details and academics about the original texts describing the dream.

On Friday May 30 1862, after sustaining his 500 oratory[91] boys four days with a promise, John Bosco delivered his now famous rendering of the great ship. Out of the 500 boys that heard the Good Night talk only four are known to have written down the dream. Two of the four boys were writing to the same friend, Frederick Oreglia, one of the original 22 Salesians of Don Bosco who was then away from the fraternity. Had it not been for his absence we probably would not have these two testimonies. A third young man wrote down the dream in his diary and a forth is recorded to have written down the dream but the document was subsequently lost. In addition to the four written testimonies, there is the oral testimony of one Cannon Bourlot. Fr. Giovanni Battista Lemoyne, in the Biographical Memoirs of Saint John Bosco, reluctantly captured Bourlot's version of the dream. Although Lemoyne was not present at the telling of the dream he later became John Bosco's official biographer. Were it not for the work of Fr. Lemoyne the two letters and the diary might not have survived, there would be no record of the fourth document, and Cannon Bourlot's testimony would be forgotten.

Summary of Scribes

John Boggero - student age 20 later became a priest. Wrote a letter on May 31, 1862 detailing the dream to Frederick Oreglia.

---

[91] Oratory is the name Don Bosco gave to the place where he and many young boys would gather for worship, sometimes without shelter. The term literally means place of prayer.

Caesar Chiala - student age 25. Wrote a letter on June 5, 1862 about the dream to Frederick Oreglia.

Dominic Ruffino – Seminarian. Wrote about the dream in his personal daily chronicle. When he died in 1865 Lemoyne inherited his chronicles.

Secundus Merlone – Seminarian who wrote down the dream. The document is lost, but is mentioned in the Biographical Memoirs of Saint John Bosco.

Canon John Mary Bourlot – Seminarian who gave his oral testimony in the oratory at least twice in a 45 year period and is documented in the Biographical Memoirs of Saint John Bosco.

Fr. Giovanni Battista Lemoyne – As early as 1864 he began recording significant things that Don Bosco said or did. After Don Bosco's death in 1888, Lemoyne was formally given the task to compile the Biographical Memoirs on Don Bosco (45 large volumes). He made copious notes and documents in preparation for the memoirs some of which remain with the Salesian order to this day. Among them is a document (referred to hereafter as the Lemoyne Documenti) that Lemoyne prepared for what he titled as *A Dream: The Two Columns*.

Controversial Points

There are five controversial issues about the dream:

1. <u>Counting Popes</u> - How many Popes did Don Bosco mention? Cannon Bourlot testifies that there are three Popes in all not two.
2. <u>Two of a Kind</u> - Is Ruffino's text a copy? Are Lemoyne's biographies accurate, especially concerning the storm and the fleet that fights for the Pope in the dream?
3. <u>Disappearing Ink</u> – Where did the images of the escort fleet, the storms and the meetings of captains come from?
4. <u>Prophetic Dream or Ordinary Parable</u> - Is the Good Night a dream or a parable? Is it prophetic or not?

What follows is an analysis of each of these controversies, which developed into the rendering used in this book.

Counting Popes

Bourlot was a cleric studying philosophy and staying at the Oratory from 1861 to 1863. He was present at the Good Night where the dream was told but did not write it down. Instead he relied on his prized memory. According to the memoirs[92], it wasn't until 1886 when Bourlot visited the Oratory that Lemoyne and Bosco heard his version of the dream. While at dinner Bourlot began reminiscing to Bosco about the old days and then recounted the dream to Don Bosco as he remembered it. Bourlot insisted that two Popes had fallen, which would make a total of three Popes since the first fall. When Bosco

---

[92] *The Biographical Memoirs of Saint John Bosco* by Fr. Giovanni Lemoyne, Salesiana Publishers, pp 109, 110

told Lemoyne, "Listen carefully to what father Bourlot is saying" Lemoyne retorted that he was well acquainted with the dream since he was in possession of the manuscripts and that he believed that there were only two Popes (one who falls and one after that). Whereupon Don Bosco told Lemoyne, "You know nothing at all!"

In 1907, nine years after Don Bosco's death, Bourlot revisited the oratory and again brought up the dream and reminded Lemoyne of what Don Bosco had said concerning the two Popes who had fallen. In the memoirs, Lemoyne credits Bourlot for his excellent memory. The three surviving manuscripts mention only one Pope who falls and is replaced. Since Secundus Merlone's manuscript is not available we cannot know if it contained any information about a second Pope falling but it is unlikely since Lemoyne did not include it in his account of the dream nor did he mention it in the section on Bourlot's points. Instead, on the issue of how many Popes fall Lemoyne wrote in the memoirs, "…which of the two versions is correct? Events may still resolve the doubt." Lemoyne is correct in deducing that there is no conclusion to be made about the number of Popes who fall. Relying on the unfolding of events for proof, as Lemoyne recommends is a wise practice that Don Bosco often employed himself writing, "He [Don Bosco], like others, waited for verification of something that had seemed to him to be a prophecy but that he chose out of prudence to present merely as a parable.[93]"

---

[93] *Don Bosco's Dreams* by Pietro Stella, translated by John Drury, Salesiana Publishers, Forward to the English Edition, p. xiv. This book sites as the original source: *Don Bosco: Religious Outlook and Spirituality*, Ch. XV sec. 5: "Don Bosco and the extraordinary," pp. 512-14

While Don Bosco's endorsement of Bourlot's testimony may seem definitive we must consider Don Bosco's purpose for saying so. It may not be for the sake of accuracy but rather for the sake of fostering healthy apprehension leading to true devotion to Christ that he called Lemoyne's attention to Bourlot's account. Don Bosco was accomplished at performing magic tricks and knew the art of misdirection. One hand leads the eye away while the other performs the necessary task to create the illusion. This misdirection was something that Don Bosco employed often, especially if it meant he could encourage the boys to deepen their devotions to Christ. Such was the case just two months prior to the telling of his Dream of the Great Ship.

On March 21, 1862 Don Bosco told of another dream[94]. This dream will help us to understand Saint Bosco's motives and methods. It was about a tall old man draped in a sheet and carrying a blue torch. The old man wandered around the Oratory grounds searching for something or someone. Finding the right boy at play he pulled a note from the folds of his sheet and handed it to the boy who paled as he read it, asking, "when?" The man told him, "Now." Then, pointing to a coffin in the passageway to the orchard continued, "Do you see that coffin? It's for you! Quick let's go!" At this point Don Bosco told the boys that they should prepare themselves because the Lord would soon call one of them to eternity. "I know who he is because I saw the whole thing. I know the boy to whom the stranger handed the note. He is here now, listening to me, but I shall tell no one until after his death. However, I'll do all I can to prepare him for a happy

---

[94] *The Biographical Memoirs of Saint John Bosco* by Fr. Giovanni Lemoyne, Salesiana Publishers, pp 76-106

death. Let each of you look after himself, for while he wonders who it is, he himself may just be the one," Don Bosco warned them. Then he added that each of them should say a minimum of one Hail Holy Queen to the Blessed Virgin Mary during the remaining three days of the feast of the Annunciation, for the sake of the boy who has to die.

When Don Bosco had finished the Good Night talk some of the boys asked privately if the one who is to die would die soon. Don Bosco cryptically replied that it would unfailingly happen before two feast days beginning with the letter 'P'. He added that it might even happen before the first of those feasts maybe even in two or three weeks.

Expectedly, this dream caused shudders among the boys there that night as they concluded that one of them would die between Easter (Pasqua) and Pentecost. Many of the boys began to exemplify model behavior. Such was the case of twelve-year-old Louis Farnasio. In the few days directly after the dream Louis pestered Don Bosco into hearing another general confession lasting several sessions, even though he had already recently made one. On the day of the first session he began to feel sick. On the last day of his confession and reception of Holy Communion, his visiting brothers, seeing his illness obtained permission to take him home for a time. On April 16, 1862 Louis Farnasio died while at home in Borgaro Torinese. His death caused a stir in the Oratory such that Don Bosco told the boys that night that they all had learned an important lesson: "Make hay while the sun shines." He added, "Let us not allow the devil to delude us into thinking we may put our conscience in order at the moment of death."

When pressed to tell whether Louis was the one, Don Bosco resolved that he would say nothing for the moment but mentioned that it was usual for boys to die in pairs – one calling the other. For this reason he encouraged the others to heed the Lord's advice: "Be ready because at an hour that you do not expect, the Son of Man will come." {Matt. 24:44] When the clerics at the Oratory pressed him, Don Bosco told them plainly that Louis was not the one. He also told them that the name of the boy who would soon be called to eternity began with the letter 'M'. Some began to conjecture that it would be Louis Marchisio, who was already seriously ill.

That year Easter fell on Sunday April 20. By April 25 some still continued their healthy apprehension while many were wondering if the prophecy would manifest. It happened unexpectedly that Victor Maestro died of a heart attack while preparing to go home. He was feeling very tired and at the doctor's recommendation took more rest. When he arranged to go home, the memoirs conclude that his plan was to escape the prophecy, thinking, "Someone is to die at the Oratory. If I go home, it can't be me. I'll have a longer [Easter] holiday and come back in perfect shape." Maestro's coffin was unusually placed on chairs in the portico overlooking the orchard just as in the dream. It also happened by surprise, or rather urgently, just as John Bosco had described.

It is interesting to note that the two initials Don Bosco gave us, 'P' and 'M' can symbolize Patter (father) and Matter (mother) for God the Father and Mary our Mother. These initials can also mean Post Mortem, meaning after death. These initials denote the message that Don Bosco gave us from the beginning of this dream. It is as if he is cryptically saying I'll tell you after the fact, or pray to the

Father with your Holy Mother's intersession. We should be careful not to overlook the mystery that Don Bosco intentionally fostered, which brought about, at least for a time, repentant hearts.

When we apply this to the Dream of the Great Ship, we see that seeking to know how many Popes fall and how many there are until the ship is moored to the columns is folly unless it leads us to deeper faith first. Don Bosco may have alluded to endorsing Bourlot's version of the dream just to rekindle interest in the story, which leads the listener to join himself with Mary and the Eucharist. The real point is to prepare your heart, to anchor yourself to Christ and to Mary. Lemoyne with the help of Caesar Chiala (one of the witnesses who penned a letter about the dream) came to the same conclusion, writing in the memoirs "Don Bosco in telling it [the dream of the Two Columns] seemed to have no other purpose than spurring the boys to pray for the Church and the Pope and fostering their devotion to the Blessed Sacrament and Mary Immaculate".

Lemoyne points out that in 1861 and 1862 the church was sorely in need of such devotions. He provides as proof the events surrounding one Jesuit priest named Charles Pasaglia. Pasaglia's intellectual pride and avarice for church positions ended him in the Roman Liberal Party with Count Cavour and the Risorgimento movement, which was aggressively seeking to establish state power. In Turin they had plotted to carry out their strategy to usurp papal power for the state during the conclave to be convened at Pius IX's death. But his Church superiors defrocked Pasaglia and he turned, unsuccessfully, to bribing several prelates into convincing the Pope to give up his rights. Then (1861) from Florence he issued a paper entitled *Pro Causa Italica* (For Case at law Italica), which promoted his views against the papal temporal power and in favor of Italian unification. Soon he discarded his clerical robes and returned to Turin acquiring the chair of moral philosophy at the Royal University.

Pasaglia founded a newspaper called *Il Mediatore,* a weekly newspaper that welcomed any priest with a grievance and led the opposition by duping unsuspecting priests into believing in dual agency for both the Church and the revolution. Other factions began to arise throughout the region, coercing support. Bishop Michael of Ariano was elected and accepted honorary presidency of these federated associations. The unrepentant bishop died nine months later in Naples. With Don Bosco's help Pasaglia recanted, at first privately. When near death Pasaglia recanted publicly, as did Nicomede Bianchi a staunch anticlerical who gave Bosco much trouble for many years previously. That the Church was under attack politically, philosophically, morally and militarily is well established. There were even several attempts made directly against Don Bosco's life. These events may all indicate John Bosco's motive for telling the dream of the Two Columns to the oratory boys.

The dream of the great ship, which followed at the heel of the prophesied death of a youth in the Oratory, and occurred during a time of great upheaval in the church and government, was well primed. Don Bosco even told the clerics of the Oratory that there would soon be two more deaths there[95]. Because of the preoccupation with death at the Oratory and the current revolution, the

---

[95] *The Biographical Memoirs of Saint John Bosco* by Fr. Giovanni Lemoyne, Salesiana Publishers, p 84

double fall of the Pope was a hot topic from the start. It was never an incidental point that was obscured over time and recently rekindled in the 20th century. Lemoyne points out that "This dream caused the boys no end of wonderment, especially regarding the two Popes. But Don Bosco volunteered no further information." This tactic, whether intentional or not, is much to the magician's code of never repeating a trick twice to the same audience. While the dream is no trick, the method of producing wonder is nevertheless, the same.

Two of a Kind

A side-by-side comparison of the Ruffino document with the Chiala letter manifests striking similarities. In fact, some sections of the two documents are completely identical. For this reason Fr. Pietro Stella concludes that Ruffino's "chronicle account is none other than the Chiala account.[96]" That is one possible and likely explanation for the origin of the Ruffino chronicle. It certainly gives reason for the identical passages. However, it does not consider the sections where they differ, a motive for copying, or the accessibility of Chiala's letter.

One could imagine that Ruffino, seeing Chiala's letter somehow, might make only slight changes if he agreed with most of its content. Such acceptance would seem to validate it all the more. Lemoyne concluded just that when he wrote in the memoirs, "All four narratives agree perfectly except the omission of some details." Yet the similarities are not enough to be conclusive. If Ruffino was copying Chiala why aren't the documents verbatim? We should also examine the differences. Take the Gospels

---

[96] *Don Bosco's Dreams* by Pietro Stella, translated by John Drury, Salesiana Publishers, p57

for example. We don't look at the similarities between the Gospels and conclude that Matthew copied from Mark[97]. Neither do we look at the differences and conclude that any one or all gospel accounts are wrong. Instead we acknowledge both similarities and differences and we conclude there is harmony between and surrounding the testimonies like musical notes that are each of a different tone yet, when played together, form a consonant chord. And there is distinction between them because of the unique qualities of their authors, who like instruments sound different as the Holy Spirit gives them utterance.

I do not mean to say that the written accounts of the dream are divinely inspired. Rather, in each case the young writers set out to chronicle the dream for their own purposes. The similarities therefore show the accuracy of the recorders efforts. It would be a fair conclusion that where the words so closely match, they are likely the very words that Don Bosco himself used. This is also within the bounds of reasonableness, is sufficient explanation for the origin of all written accounts, and lends rationale for both similarities and slight differences between the texts.

There are also a few points that refute the idea that Ruffino copied Chiala. One should consider that Ruffino, himself an eyewitness to the Good Night talk, would have no motive for copying Chiala. Additionally, he would not have had access to the letter until weeks after the event, a fact that contradicts Lemoyne's observation of the docu-

---

[97] Some scholarship, known as Marcan Priority and rooted in nineteenth century Germany, does conjecture that Mathew and Luke copied from Mark. Its flaw consists mainly in the elements not found in Mark, leading to the necessity of a conveniently missing document commonly referred to as Q. Some scholars conjecture that Q is not a document but the apostolic traditions of the Church. In which case no apostle is copying but all are recording as it has been handed down to them.

ments. "...Don Bosco's narration was taken down immediately and as accurately as possible.[98]" Since the accounts were taken down immediately, we can expect that Ruffino would have written the account in his daily chronicle before the June 5 date on Chiala's letter. It would not have been possible for Ruffino to see the letter before June 5 since Chiala states that he did not write until the moment of the letters date.

"I have kept it to myself until today, convinced from day to day that you would be back in Turin; but since your absence is continually prolonged, I could no longer hold back from writing you.[99]"

Furthermore, the June 6 – 7 postmark makes it impossible to have had access to the letter to copy until days, even weeks later. That could only happen once Oreglia would have received it and returned to the oratory with it[100]. We know for certain that He was back at the oratory by July 21, 1862, as there is a letter from Don Bosco in Lanzo to Chevalier Oreglia and received at the oratory. That is almost two months between the telling of the dream and a definitive time that Oreglia and the Chiala letter were available in the oratory. If Ruffino did not write down the event in his chronicle sooner than that, it calls into question both the purpose of the chronicle and Ruffino's sincerity in keeping it altogether. Chiala's comment that he kept it to himself also dispenses with the reverse; the idea that Chiala copied from Ruffino (albeit a more reasonable assertion). The only respectable and fair

---

[98] *The Biographical Memoirs of Saint John Bosco* by Fr. Giovanni Lemoyne, Salesiana Publishers, p 109
[99] *Don Bosco's Dreams* by Pietro Stella, translated by John Drury, Salesiana Publishers, footnotes pp 78&79
[100] It would be of value to check the Oratory register and see when Oreglia returned, however these records are not available to this author presently.

conclusion then, is that Ruffino and Chiala penned their accounts separately but with remarkable similarities. Indeed, there were more remarkable events than that frequently taking place at the oratory.

<u>Disappearing Ink</u>

As mentioned at the beginning of this chapter in the section defining the scribes of this dream, Fr. Lemoyne began his biographical work on Don Bosco in 1864 (two years after the dream). He wasn't officially given the responsibility of documenting the memoirs until Don Bosco's death in 1888. As you can imagine Lemoyne collected original documents and created numerous intermediate writings, which he used to compile the Biographical Memoirs. One such document exists as a precursor to pages 107–113 in volume VII of the Biographical Memoirs of Saint John Bosco. The document is printed[101] and splits into two columns where the dream narration begins. It also contains notes in the margins, which show Fr. Lemoyne's editorial process on the narration portion. Also printed into the document is the closing remark: "The clerics Boggero and Ruffino, and a young man, Chiala, who later became a priest, wrote down this dream, thus leaving us with these *three*[102] valuable documents. " Yet when this document is transposed to the final book, Lemoyne records that there were *four* manuscripts and mentions all transcribers by name, including Merlone.

---

[101] This author has not seen the actual document but relies on the material presented in Fr. Pietro Stella's book, *Don Bosco's Dreams*, translated by John Drury, Salesiana Publishers, p82, footnote 187

[102] *Don Bosco's Dreams* by Pietro Stella, translated by John Drury, Salesiana Publishers, p84, emphasis added.

Admittedly, Fr. Lemoyne's biographical work on Don Bosco as a whole is editorial and the dream of the two columns is no exception. Not being an eyewitness himself, Fr. Lemoyne apparently took from the four written accounts that were available to him and combined them into one homogenous story. This is an understandable thing to do when you already have mountainous volumes of biographical information to summarize. When you examine the dream account in the Biographical Memoirs certain sections stand out since they have no counterpart in the three surviving original manuscripts. These parts are also penned in Lemoyne's handwriting in the margins of the Lemoyne documenti. The parts that stand out are the storm, the meeting of captains and the fleet of escort ships. The easy solution is to say that Lemoyne invented these sections but there is no way of being certain since we do not have all four texts that Lemoyne testified he had; namely the Merlone document.

In his book, Don Bosco's Dreams, noted historian Fr. Pietro Stella writes, "the evening talk of May 30, 1862, did not purport to evoke images of one fleet against another." In other words the ships never had a meaning of representing individual churches or bishops in communion with Rome but they always represented human beings, persecutions and the nations, and the great ship always represented the whole church with the Pope at its head, and not the Holy See. Since these concepts are difficult to find in the surviving three accounts, Fr. Stella concludes "The idea of a fleet faithful to the Pope and symbolizing local churches in communion with Rome may have been suggested to Father Lemoyne by comments in the Boggero account.[103]" Indeed the Boggero letter mentions:

"But on the big ship there quickly appears a new Pope, who routs all the already tottering ships..."

And again:

"Then one saw many of the small ships, some that had fought for this one, others far away that had retreated for fear of the battle, scurry to the columns and attach themselves..."

To the contrary, the fact that Boggero does distinguish between ships that had fought for the Flagship and those that remained far away clearly expresses that such a concept was not alien to the talk that evening. We see evidence of this in the confusion of battle described in both the Chiala and Ruffino accounts:

"Then great disorder breaks out. All the ships that so far had been battling the ship captained by the Pope scatter, flee, collide with one another. Some founder and try to sink the others. Those at a distance keep prudently back until all the remains of all the demolished ships have sunk into the depths of the sea, and then they vigorously proceed to those two columns." ~ Ruffino

"Then total disorder breaks out over the whole surface of the sea. All the ships that so far had been battling the Pope's ship scatter, flee, and collide with one another, some foundering and trying to sink the others." ~ Chiala

---

[103] *Don Bosco's Dreams* by Pietro Stella, translated by John Drury, Salesiana Publishers, p58

The ones that founder have no need to sink the others if the others are sinking also. Clearly there are some ships in the middle of the battle that are not sinking. These would be the ones that are fighting with the flagship. These may represent individual Catholic churches or even those protestant churches that are not with the enemy yet are not in full communion with Rome. Beyond this there is yet another group of ships that don't even get into the fight. These would be the neutral nations or the catechumen who, in waiting, long to join the Church. Thus the various ships having various degrees of union with the Pope's ship reflect both the Church and the world. How fitting since the Church in relation to the world was the very topic of the Second Vatican Council. That is something Lemoyne could not have known and therefore could not have added to the texts.

What remains difficult to prove through the available original documents is the conference of captains. One glaring omission in all the recorded stories including Lemoyne's is that no specific mention is made of the Pope's auxiliary ships or captains fixing themselves to the two pillars. We would expect this from a group of captains who are of one accord with their leader, who has done as much by example. Additionally, having a fleet or flotilla of auxiliary ships would seem to deny the unity of the Catholic Church, which has long been referred to as the bark of Peter; a single ship. Yet the Second Vatican Council made it clear that "the bishops who, under the appointment of the Holy Spirit, succeeded in the place of the apostles, feed and rule individually, as true shepherds, the particular flock assigned to them.[104]"

---

[104] Dogmatic Constitution *Pastor Aeternus* on the Church of Christ (1870)

Another explanation why the auxiliary ships are not specifically mentioned to tie up at the pillars is that the Pope's captains are never mentioned to have returned to their ships after the second council. It may be that the success of the second council secures the captains aboard the great ship for the duration of the journey. Symbolically, this could mean that although the Bishops rule independently they are still one with the Pope in acting as the person of Christ. As a point of fact *Lumen Gentium*, the second of the constitutions of Vatican II, defines the unique hierarchical and ministerial role of the Priest in relation to the common but royal role of the faithful.

"Though they differ from one another in essence and not only in degree, the common priesthood of the faithful and the ministerial or hierarchical priesthood are nonetheless interrelated: each of them in its own special way is a participation in the one priesthood of Christ. The ministerial priest, by the sacred power he enjoys, teaches and rules the priestly people; acting in the person of Christ, he makes present the eucharistic sacrifice, and offers it to God in the name of all the people. But the faithful, in virtue of their royal priesthood, join in the offering of the Eucharist. They likewise exercise that priesthood in receiving the sacraments, in prayer and thanksgiving, in the witness of a holy life, and by self-denial and active charity."
Lumen Gentium, Section 10 - 105

This definition is one that binds priests and laity in the one priesthood of Christ, through the Eucharistic sacrifice. This is the very point that John Bosco was making by depicting the Church's stability amidst the turbulent waters of the world, as dependant on anchoring first to the Eucharist, then to Mary.

Another supporting reference to a fleet comes to us from the original draft of Caesar Chiala. In the section informing us about the enemy ships that sink into the sea there is a correction made and the original words are still legible. Instead of calling them "demolished ships" he began referring to them as "that flotilla". This term also appears in the Lemoyne document near the beginning.

"This stately vessel is shielded by a flotilla escort. Winds and waves are with the enemy."

Did Lemoyne get the term from the Chiala original and expand on it or did it come from the Merlone original? Without the Merlone document we cannot know with one hundred percent certainty. It is doubtful that "the testimony of Canon Bourlot, only oral in all likelihood, might have also been the source of Lemoyne's additions to the documenti, [105]" as Fr. Stella emphasizes. For reasons mentioned in the preceding section Lemoyne probably considered Bourlot's testimony as tenuous. Lemoyne's self professed reluctance to accept Bourlot's testimony is evidence enough that Lemoyne chose none of Bourlot's testimony to be part of the final redaction. Lemoyne may have decided to make note of Bourlot's argument in the Biographical Memoirs and set it apart from the redaction out of respect for Don Bosco who told him to "listen carefully". Then again, Lemoyne makes it clear that Bourlot's rendition was just one opinion among many "endless arguments and conflicting explanations" circulat-

---

[105] *Don Bosco's Dreams* by Pietro Stella, translated by John Drury, Salesiana Publishers, p60

ing at the time. The missing letter written by Secundus Merlone is a far more probable source. Fr. Stella speculates "Perhaps they [the documents by Secundus Merlone] might have helped us clear up our perplexity about Lemoyne's marginal additions to the text of the documenti." Common sense elucidates that Lemoyne is adding to his already penned compilation some testimony of which he became aware after the fact.

I would like to offer you what I consider to be the most convincing evidence that the source of the added testimony was Merlone's document. The evidence is the other documents that Merlone wrote and which Lemoyne incorporated into the memoirs elsewhere. Through these recordings we are able to evaluate the quality and depth of Merlone's chronography, which will explain why his could be the only testimony with such specifics, and consequently why Lemoyne added them to his own notes.

In *Counting Popes*, we examined another dream of Don Bosco's, surrounding the events of the death of one of the oratory boys. In that dream Don Bosco witnessed an ominous looking man, dressed in sheet enter the courtyard, find the right young boy, and hand him a note. Fr. Lemoyne recorded that dream in the memoirs from two surviving original written accounts. The first document is written by Fr. John Bonetti, the other is by Secundus Merlone, the very same one who penned the missing document on the dream of the great ship. This establishes that Lemoyne made prior use of Merlone's documentation and gives us a chance to examine Lemoyne's editorial process. It also gives us the opportunity to examine Merlone's writing style and compare it with the marginal notes in the documenti that became the Biographical Memoirs of Saint John Bosco.

A side-by-side comparison of the Bonetti and Merlone documents reveals that Lemoyne mixed the two accounts and did paraphrase occasionally. For instance, the Bonetti account starts out, "Imagine you see the boys of the house at recreation, some jumping and running, others coming and going." Whereas Lemoyne enters in the document, "Try to picture yourselves the Oratory at recreation time loud with happy, boisterous youngsters." So we must acknowledge that Lemoyne was in the habit of paraphrasing but there is no indication that he added content purely of his own making. Also, Lemoyne seems to favor the Merlone document, which is considerably more descriptive and verbose. For example, Bonetti describes the stranger:

"At that point there emerges a character who takes a few turns around the courtyard, then comes under the portico, approaches a boy who is there in a corner, and hands him a note."

In contrast Merlone describes the same character:

"Looking over there I saw a specter: tall, with a wide forehead, deeply sunken eyes, a long white beard, and a few white locks of hair thinly falling about his shoulders. He appeared to be wrapped in a winding-sheet, which he held close to his body with his left hand. In his right hand he held a dark blue flaming torch. He walked with slow grave steps…"

Seeing that Merlone is far more detailed in his chronicle than Bonetti, we expect that he was also far more detailed in chronicling the Dream of the Great Two Columns. If the marginal notes in the documenti are Merlone's, is it any wonder that his is the only testimony that includes such detail about storms and councils? Clearly Merlone is a cut above the rest as a chronicler. He is most defensibly the sole chronicler who made note of the details of the storm and the councils. With this in mind, Merlone becomes the most logical and likely source of Lemoyne's handwritten notes in the margin of his Documenti, and also the most valuable of the four writers and witnesses. It is possible that Merlone's rendition still exists in his own handwriting but it would not likely be in the Salesian archives since Merlone was ordained a priest in a different order. Discovering his personal notes would answer many questions about this dream as well as other visions that Don Bosco shared.

From this anomaly and from other aforementioned details it should be possible to reconstruct Lemoyne's editorial process and in so doing, express the reasonableness of this theory that Lemoyne became aware of new facts only after having written what he thought was a final draft compilation of the original texts.

In conclusion of this section I would like to offer the reader a scenario of conjecture; one possible scenario for what transpired with Lemoyne's research and writing:

On May 30, 1862 Don Bosco tells the 500 oratory boys and clerics of the dream of the great ship. That night or within the week Dominic Ruffino records the details of the dream in his personal memoirs. The next day, May 31, 1862 John Boggero wrote Frederick Oreglia about the dream. One week after the telling, Caesar Chiala writes Fredrick Oreglia with the purpose of describing the dream. Around this same time cleric Secundus Merlone writes the dream out, presumably in his diary[106] but possibly in a letter. In 1864 Fr. Lemoyne meets Don Bosco for the first time and considers him a man of exceptional holiness. Like many people who were in Don Bosco's presence, Fr. Lemoyne began to chronicle his experiences with him. He begins gathering information from eyewitnesses on topics concerning events prior to their meeting. Among the items he collects are the Chiala and Boggero letters, from addressee Fredrick (Chevalier) Oreglia. One year later, in 1865 Dominic Ruffino dies leaving his personal effects in the charge of Fr. Lemoyne. Among Ruffino's possessions are his memoirs. From this chronicle Lemoyne copies[107] the account of the dream. Fr. Lemoyne begins comparing the three documents and compiling them into a single account. This work he saves with the rest of his documentation on Don Bosco, noting that there are three valuable documents. In 1872 just before returning to his home diocese, Fr. Secundus Merlone makes his diary account of the dream available to Fr. Lemoyne, who hastily writes its details in the margins of his own documents. The original diary he returns to Fr. Merlone. In 1886 Cannon Bourlot visits the Oratory and Don Bosco encourages Fr. Lemoyne to take note of his points on the Pope who falls. In 1888 Don Bosco dies and Fr. Lemoyne is officially charged with the responsibility to compile the complete work of this saints life. In 1907 Cannon Bourlot returns to the oratory reminding Fr. Lemoyne of Don Bosco's recognition of his points on the Pope who is struck and dies. Fr. Lemoyne, having already

---

[106] It was common practice for young men to keep a diary for the purposes of assisting in examining one's conscience and relationship with Christ. It's the kind of thing that clergy recommended then. There were also several people including Ruffino who had the duty of recording Don Bosco's orations.

[107] This copybook document along with the two letters retrieved from Fredrick Oreglia remains in the Salesians care to this day.

compiled the four manuscripts on the dream finds no place in it for Cannon Bourlot's observations but having been persuaded by Bourlot, includes the events of his rendition in subsequent paragraphs of the Memoirs. When transposing his documents to the final draft of the Biographical Memoirs, Fr. Lemoyne refreshes the compiled dream redaction to include the notes copied from Fr. Merlone's records and updates the section regarding the number of "valuable documents" to four.

Prophetic Dream or Ordinary Parable?

There is much debate over whether or not John Bosco's Good Night talk on May 30, 1862 was a dream. Some may consider the stakes of this debate high. For if it is not a dream, they think, what prophetic authority does it have in the world? It is not enough for it to be simply clairvoyant[108], they argue, but it must also be prophetic[109]. If Don Bosco simply perceived something that others could not, this is tantamount to contriving the story. The camp on the pro-Parable side would say, then its relevance is that of its day only. The camp on the pro-dream side, having the motive of proving the story's futuristically prophetic relevance, argues therefore that it is a dream. This is a reactionary position to take and not necessarily an advantageous one.

As regards categorizing the dream of the two columns, there are at least three types of Clairvoyant dreams or visions, which John Bosco experienced and perhaps assimilated into parables. First there are those that are like a snapshot of the soul. These kinds of dreams are meant

---

[108] Clairvoyance is the knowledge of something that is not perceptible through the five senses. It may include a person or group's intention or disposition, or the likely outcome of one or more future events.
[109] Prophecy is specifically the foreknowledge of one or more future events.

for the spiritual growth of the individual. Then there are the kinds of dreams that are like the bulk of the ones that Don Bosco shared with us. These kinds of dreams are ministerial or of a missionary purpose. That is, they serve to evangelize and convert a community. Most of the dreams that St. John Bosco experienced helped him to lead the youths of the oratory to a closer relationship with God. They were for the spiritual development of a specific group of boys and many times John knew which ones in particular. Lastly there are the kinds of dreams that foretold the future, sometimes for kings, the Pope or for the church. All of these types are clairvoyant and to some degree prophetic. That is they reveal something about the person or group that is otherwise not perceptible, either in that present moment or for the near or distant future.

How do we know if this dream of the two columns is a message from God? This is an important question that is best answered through time. Even Don Bosco "waited for verification of something that had seemed to him to be a prophecy but that he chose out of prudence to present merely as a parable.[110]" Since only God can see the beginning from the end, only God can know the hearts of men and predict future events with one hundred percent accuracy. The devils and demons have access to knowledge but they do not know everything from beginning to end. So when a devil attempts to deceive, the lie is known in the end when it is unfulfilled. In other words a tree is known by its fruit. So it is important that every word of prophecy be fulfilled exactly as revealed in order for us to

---

[110] *Don Bosco's Dreams* by Pietro Stella, translated by John Drury, Salesiana Publishers, Forward to the English Edition, p. xiv. This book sites as the original source: *Don Bosco: Religious Outlook and Spirituality*, Ch. XV sec. 5: "Don Bosco and the extraordinary," pp. 512-14

know that it is valid beyond any doubt. One is permitted to have faith in private revelation but at the same time messages and reasoning from that revelation must not contradict faith. So if by reason or by the unfolding of history some of the details of a given prophecy are exposed as untrue, the prophecy is invalid.

But what do we make of recorded prophecies like Jonah's warning to Nineveh that God would destroy it. Initially Jonah's message from God was well received by the king of that city. Subsequently the dire fasting of every creature in that city so begged for mercy that God granted it and the city was spared. Now, one can say that the prophecy was not true because the town should have been destroyed or one can praise the mercy of God. This brings us to a delicate point regarding John Bosco's dream of the two columns. The order of Popes and assassination attempts is not perfectly congruous with what is historically known. According to the rule, this would give us reason to doubt the dreams authenticity. Else we would have to consider the ream to be more a warning contingent on our actions, much like the second and third messages of Fatima.

Also, we should consider the accuracy of the recordings, especially since John Bosco did not himself pen the words we have of the dream. But we may hold the dream to be divinely granted since many parts of it are genuinely discernable as prophetic and still hold the records of it in question specifically where they differ with historical reality. Any inaccuracy attributed to these recordings of the dream is certainly due to the limitations of the recorders or even the messenger but not the message as divinely given. Short of dreaming the same dream as God once granted to the prophet Daniel (Dan 2:19-23), we may never know. Since, the events speak for themselves and the other dreams and prophesies of Don Bosco have been spot on, there is no reason to believe that this dream is any different, only that those recording it did their best to repeat it all and in proper order. If you play a game of Telegraph or Telephone[111] you will see how easy it is to mix up the order of events.

The fact that the recordings of the dream differ around the number of Popes and their order actually does coincide with the conflicting historical evidence and conspiracy theories such that no one really knows for sure what happened. In other words, the scribes of the dream argue exactly where historical reality is confusing. Insomuch as this, the dream is not in error because it reflects a truth on a sub textual level. Fr. Lemoyne made a similar determination writing, "We shall conclude by saying that Caesar Chiala – as he himself told us – and the three above mentioned clerics [Ruffino, Boggero, Merlone] took this dream as a genuine vision and prophesy, even though Don Bosco in telling it seemed to have no other purpose than spurring the boys to pray for the Church and the Pope and fostering their devotion to the Blessed Sacrament and Mary Immaculate."[112]

I have outlined the evidence on all sides; pro-parable, pro-dream and dream-parable synthesis:

---

[111] A detailed story is provided in writing for one member of a group who is given time to read it once. He must then privately repeat the story and all its details to another person who will in turn repeat the story to another. The story is repeated over and over again till it reaches the last person who repeats it to the whole group. Then the original story is read aloud for comparison. Experience shows that verbal communication in our time is less developed than in previous centuries and millenniums.
[112] *The Biographical Memoirs of Saint John Bosco* by Fr. Giovanni Lemoyne, Salesiana Publishers, New Rochelle, New York, 1972, p110

Evidence on the Pro-Parable Side:
1. Caesar Chiala records in his letter that Don Bosco said, "I will tell you a fable, a simile."
2. Likewise Ruffino records it as a "fable or simile."
3. It appears to be inspired by the great battle of Lepanto[113].

Evidence on the Pro-Dream Side:
1. Boggero writes near the end of his letter, "What I think is that it is one of his usual dreams."
2. The fact that it took Fr. John Bosco four days to fulfill his promise of a Goodnight story may at first seem to indicate that it took him that long to conceive of it. However, John Bosco expressed elsewhere in the memoirs that he often experienced restless sleep some nights before receiving spiritual help in the form of dream images. It is likely that he made the promise because of growing awareness, and restlessness.

Evidence of Dream-Parable Synthesis:
Fr. Lemoyne, who was not present at the telling of the Good Night in question, but had occasion to speak with Don Bosco about it, records it as a both a dream and a parable.

The latter may be the closest thing to right as we can assess. It may have been a dream that Don Bosco converted to a parable, or it may have been a parable he was contemplating that crept into his dreams. Regardless, Don Bosco is a man whose wake and dream states were both permeated by the supernatural. For he saw visions when awake and when sleeping often sensed the world as if conscious. You might say he was a dream walker or walking dreamer. All the concerns he had for his minis-

---

[113] See page 24, Basic Thesis

try, society and the Church were evident in his speech and in his tales of visions and dreams. Many others who knew him told similar things about him. There is such a multitude of mystical stories surrounding Don Bosco that modern authors are moved to write things like; "In Don Bosco's dreams spirituality and social concern are blended together and are of one piece. Here is genuine Christianity.[114]" So whether it is a dream or parable its predictive qualities withstand and outstand just like the man himself. The better position to assume in this debate is that whether or not it is dream, a parable or both, it is remains intertwined with the supernatural.

Conclusions About the Dream Texts

It is clear that Fr. Lemoyne combined the various manuscripts into one account. He did not manifest his reasons for doing this, however it does give the reader a single, proximate experience to the actual event. It might even be valuable to attempt to reconstruct parts of the Merlone letter by comparing Lemoyne's redaction against the original letters. What Fr. Stella identifies as glosses may turn out to be further evidence of the missing letter. Lemoyne attests that there were four letters,

"The clerics Boggero, Merlone, and Ruffino, and a layman, Caesar Chiala, wrote down this dream. We have their manuscripts; two were written on May 31st and two much later. All

---

[114] *Don Bosco's Dreams* by Pietro Stella, translated by John Drury, Salesian Publishers, Forward to the English Edition, p. xiv. This book sites as the original source: The forward by Dr. Morton Kelsey on pp. xxxii – xxxvi of Brown, Eugene M., ed. *Dreams, Visions & Prophesies of Don Bosco*. New Rochelle: Don Bosco, 1986. 62 Dreams selected from the Biographical Memoirs of Don Bosco with the introductions of Lemoyne et al.; with a topical index.

four narratives agree perfectly except for the omission of some details."

According to Fr. Stella's book, Boggero's letter is dated May 31; Chiala's is dated June 5. That leaves either Ruffino's or Merlone's as the other document written on May 31. Since Ruffino's is taken from his chronicle entry, it is likely to be the one created on May 31, but we can't know for sure. Because Chiala's letter is dated but not on may 31 it must be one of the two that Lemoyne says were written "much later". Lemoyne apparently considers a week to be a considerable amount of time to lapse before chronicling such details. By deduction, either the Merlone letter is the second letter reported to have been written on the May 31, or else it is paired with the Chiala letter written on June 5. Either way, it is not removed any great period of time from the event. No matter what month or day, and without any doubt, all of the documents in question were composed in 1862[115]. This would further distinguish Merlone's letter with greater credibility than Bourlot's oral testimony since Bourlot didn't tell Fr. Lemoyne until 1886, 24 years after the fact.

Clearly the work that Fr. Lemoyne labored to produce was done so with the kind of integrity that follows common sense and prudence. And so Lemoyne's document remains a major contribution, an insightful commentary, and trustworthy source of the documentation on Don Bosco's Dream of the two columns. Since we have established good cause to trust Fr. Lemoyne we can also trust the not so mysterious additions of texts to the

---

[115] According to Fr. Stella's footnote 136 on pg81 of *Don Bosco's Dreams*, Salesiana Publishers 1996: Lemoyne's copybook sample of Ruffino's diary, which is in the Central Salesian Archives, is among those memoirs Lemoyne collected from years ranging 1862 – 1863.

documenti. Conclusively, the sections on the storm and councils, which Fr. Lemoyne included in his redaction, are acceptable, if not by the other evidence mentioned earlier in this chapter, then by his good testimony. To exclude them would be to commit the very redaction errors that the countering criticism seeks to uncover. So we have determined that the three surviving original documents, as well as the Lemoyne documenti with all its handwritten notes are each unique and trustworthy records of the Good Night that Don Bosco told on May 30, 1862.

- RESOURCES -

The 200 Day March
Dream of St. John Bosco
(*May 24 - June 24, 1873*)

It was a dark night, and men could no longer find their way back to their own countries. Suddenly a most brilliant light shone in the sky, illuminating their way as at high noon. At that moment from the Vatican came forth, as in procession, a multitude of men and women, young children, monks, nuns, and priests, and at their head was the Pope. But a furious storm broke out, somewhat dimming that light, as if light and darkness were locked in battle. Meanwhile the long procession reached a small square littered with dead and wounded, many of whom cried for help. The ranks of the procession thinned considerably. After a two hundred day march, all realized that they were no longer in Rome. In dismay they swarmed about the Pontiff to protect him and minister to him in his needs.

At that moment two angels appeared, bearing a banner, which they presented to the Supreme Pontiff, saying: "Take the banner of her who battles and routs the most powerful armies on earth. Your enemies have vanished: with tears and sighs your children plead for your return." One side of the banner bore the inscription: Regina sine labe concepta [Queen conceived without sin], and the other side read: Auxilium Christianorum_[Help of Christians]. The Pontiff accepted the banner gladly, but he became distressed to see how few were his followers.

But the two angels went on: "Go now, comfort your children. Write to your brothers scattered throughout the world that men must reform their lives. This cannot be achieved unless the bread of the Divine Word is broken among the peoples. Teach children their catechism and preach detachment from earthly things. The time has come," the two angles concluded, "when the poor will evangelize the world. Priests shall be sought among those who wield the hoe, the spade, and the hammer, as David prophesied: 'God lifted the poor man from the fields to place him on the throne of His people.'"

On hearing this, the Pontiff moved on, and the ranks began to swell. Upon reaching the Holy City, the Pontiff wept at the sight of its desolate citizens, for many of them were no longer. He then entered St. Peter's and intoned the Te Deum, to which a chorus of angels responded, singing: Gloria in excelsis Deo et in terra pax hominibus bonae voluntatis [Glory to God in the highest, and peace on earth to men of good will.] When the song was over, all darkness vanished and a blazing sun shone.

The population had declined greatly in the cities and in the countryside; the land was mangled as if by a hurricane and hailstorm, and people sought each other, deeply moved, and saying: Est Deus in Israel [There is a God in Israel].

From the start of the exile until the intoning of the Te Deum, the sun rose 200 times. All the events described covered a period of 400 days.

Interpretations of the 200 Day March

Dark Night
  Misunderstanding, lack of understanding or knowledge or suppressed spiritual knowledge. John 1:5

A most brilliant light
The First Vatican Council.

High noon
  No shadows, darkness is gone. Direct sunlight only, no allusions. Complete understanding and truth. The path or the way is completely illuminated and visible.

Procession
  Although this vision depicts the Pope proceeding from the Vatican, Pope Pius IX considered himself imprisoned there when the Italian Nationalists seized it. This procession may be the period of time when communication from Pius IX came exclusively from the Vatican since he was detained there.

Small Square
  A clearing where men gather. Four corners indicate an earthly dimension. May be a reference to Revelation chapter twelve, the city of God, the new Jerusalem is laid out like a square. The new Jerusalem is the Church.

No longer in Rome
  Not following the Pope or the directives of the Church. The people had by virtually unanimous vote joined the Italian Unification, which usurped the Papal States.

Minister to the Pontiff
Implies the Pope is in need possibly injured or does not have the support of the people.

Two Angels
Two is the number of witness. Messengers from God. Divine intervention for the sake of mankind.

Banner
Mission, purpose, dedication, identity, the cause for which we fight, the name under which we fight. Mary the Immaculate Conception. Pope Pius IX pronounced the Immaculate Conception of Mary on December 8th 1854 (19 years prior to this prophecy). He defined that, "in the first instance of her conception, by a singular privilege and grace granted by God, in view of the merits of Jesus Christ, the Savior of the human race, was preserved exempt from all stain of original sin." On November 27, 1830 Catherine Laboure' had a vision of The Immaculate Virgin Mary who charged her with the mission to mint a medal with an image on both sides. This she did through her confessor in 1832. The front side of the medal bears the image of the Immaculate Virgin Mary and the phrase "O Mary, conceived without sin, pray for us who have recourse to thee". The backside of the medal depicts twelve stars, representing the apostles, the first members of the church. These stars are surrounding the letter M, which stands for Mary. In this way the message on the backside of the medal ensures us that Mary is the help of all Christians.

A God in Israel
It may come to mind that Israel became a nation again in 1948, and that seems proof that this prophecy pertains to the twentieth century. However, Israel means the "Chil-

dren of Israel" (Jacob), which refers to his descendants not just by blood but also by covenant. According to the New Covenant established by Jesus, Israel refers to the Church. So the phrase "God is in Israel" is an acknowledgement that God is truly present in the Catholic Church. What is being prophesied is that people will truly turn to the Church and acknowledge the Eucharist as Christ.

Whole event is 400 days

The prophesy encompasses period of time which is a little over one year.

200 days from exile until to Te Deum

When the Holy See officially recognized the nation of Italy with Rome as its capitol, Pope Pius IX was finally able to visit the Basilica of Saint John Lateran on the opposite side of Rome from the Vatican. The Te Deum is part of the Divine Office but is also sung in thanksgiving for special blessing. Here Pius IX is depicted giving thanks for release from his imprisonment in the Vatican.

Conclusion

Based on the many references to images found in 1800's it is clear that this dream relates to that time period and to Pope Pius IX. The reason these images in this dream so strongly match real events may have to do with the fact that it is dated three years after the events it signifies. We may account for the resemblance to the Third Secret of Fatima (44 years later) in the observation that History seems to repeat itself.

Litany of the Blessed Virgin Mary (Litany of Loreto)

V. Lord, have mercy on us.
R. *Christ, have mercy on us.*

V. Lord, have mercy on us. Christ hear us.
R. *Christ, graciously hear us.*

God, the Father of Heaven, *have mercy on us*
God, the Son, Redeemer of the world, *have mercy on us*
God, the Holy Spirit, *have mercy on us*
Holy Trinity, One God, *have mercy on us*

Holy Mary, *pray for us*
Holy Mother of God, *pray for us*
Holy Virgin of virgins, *pray for us*
Mother of Christ, *pray for us*
Mother of divine grace, *pray for us*
Mother most pure, *pray for us*
Mother most chaste, *pray for us*
Mother inviolate, *pray for us*
Mother undefiled, *pray for us*
Mother most amiable, *pray for us*
Mother most admirable, *pray for us*
Mother of good counsel, *pray for us*
Mother of our Creator, *pray for us*
Mother of our Savior, *pray for us*
Virgin most prudent, *pray for us*
Virgin most venerable, *pray for us*
Virgin most renowned, *pray for us*
Virgin most powerful, *pray for us*
Virgin most merciful, *pray for us*
Virgin most faithful, *pray for us*
Mirror of justice, *pray for us*

Seat of wisdom, *pray for us*
Cause of our joy, *pray for us*
Spiritual vessel, *pray for us*
Vessel of honor, *pray for us*
Singular vessel of devotion, *pray for us*
Mystical rose, *pray for us*
Tower of David, *pray for us*
Tower of ivory, *pray for us*
House of gold, *pray for us*
Ark of the covenant, *pray for us*
Gate of Heaven, *pray for us*
Morning star, *pray for us*
Health of the sick, *pray for us*
Refuge of sinners, *pray for us*
Comforter of the afflicted, *pray for us*
Help of Christians, *pray for us*
Queen of Angels, *pray for us*
Queen of Patriarchs, *pray for us*
Queen of Prophets, *pray for us*
Queen of Apostles, *pray for us*
Queen of Martyrs, *pray for us*
Queen of Confessors, *pray for us*
Queen of Virgins, *pray for us*
Queen of all Saints, *pray for us*
Queen conceived without Original Sin, *pray for us*
Queen assumed into Heaven, *pray for us*
Queen of the most holy rosary, *pray for us*
Queen of Peace, *pray for us*

Lamb of God, who takest away the sins of the world,
Spare us, O Lord.

Lamb of God, who takest away the sins of the world,
Graciously hear us O Lord.

Lamb of God, who takest away the sins of the world,
Have mercy on us.

V. Pray for us, O holy Mother of God.
R. That we may be made worthy of the promises of Christ.

Let us pray:
Grant, we beseech Thee, O Lord God, unto us Thy servants, that we may rejoice in continual health of mind and body; and, by the glorious intercession of blessed Mary ever Virgin, may be delivered from present sadness, and enter into the joy of Thine eternal gladness. Through Christ our Lord.

Amen.

- BIBLIOGRAPHY -

Address on the Dreams of Saint John Bosco and Especially the "Dream" of the Two Columns, Fr. Mendl, transcript of lecture, Columbus Ohio, approximately 1997

The Biographical Memoirs of Saint John Bosco by Fr. Giovanni Lemoyne, Salesiana Publishers, New Rochelle, New York, 1972

Memoirs of the Oratory of Saint Francis de Sales from 1815 to 1855 The Autobiography Of Saint John Bosco, Don Bosco Publications New Rochelle, New York, 1989

Catechism of the Catholic Church, Concacan Inc. – Libreria Editrice Vaticana, 1994, Publications Service, Canadian Conference of Catholic Bishops, Ottawa (Ontario)

Catholic News Agency, Aug. 09, 2004

Don Bosco's Dreams by Pietro Stella, translated by John Drury, Salesiana Publishers, 1996

God's Choice – Pope Benedict XVI and the Future of the Catholic Church, Harper Collins, George Weigel, 2005

Forty Dreams of Saint John Bosco, Tan Books and Publishers Inc., Rockford, Illinois, 1996

John Paul II is History's Champion Saintmaker by Cathy Lynn Grossman USA Today, 2005

Memory and Identity, John Paul II, Rizzoli International Publications, Inc., New York, N.Y. 2005

New American Bible, Confraternity of Christian Doctrine, Washington D.C., 1991, 1986, 1970

The Oxford Dictionary of Popes by J.N.D. Kelly, Oxford University Press 1986

Priest as Victim, Bishop Fulton Sheen, approximately 1970, KeeptheFaih.org.

Priest as Victim, Bishop Fulton Sheen, approximately 1970, Saint Joseph Communications.

The Ratzinger Interview, Joseph Cardinal Ratzinger with Raymond Arroyo, EWTN Home Video, Alabama, Summer 2003

Revised Standard Version of the Bible, Division of Christian Education of the National Council of the Churches of Christ in the United States of America, 1996

Spirit of the Liturgy, Ignatius Press, 2000

vatican.va/phome_en.htm; Gaudium et Spes, Message of Fatima, Conversation With Sister Maria Lucia Of Jesus And The Immaculate Heart, Address Of Cardinal Angelo Sodano Regarding The "Third Part" Of The Secret Of Fatima, Meditation with the Italian Bishops from the Policlinico Gemelli, Insegnamenti, Tertio Millennio Adveniente, homily, May 11, 1991.